# DEMOCRATS

DO THE
DUMBEST
THINGS™

# DEMOCRATS

## DO THE DUMBEST THINGS™

## Bill Crawford

RENAISSANCE BOOKS

*Los Angeles*

Library of Congress Catalog Card Number: 00-101346
ISBN: 1-58063-112-6

10 9 8 7 6 5 4 3 2 1

*Design by Lee Fukui*

Published by Renaissance Books
Distributed by St. Martin's Press
Manufactured in the United States of America
First Edition

Dedicated to the
wisdom (and patience) of
the American voter

# ACKNOWLEDGMENTS

**Thanks to my coauthor "Deep Throat,"** who wishes to remain anonymous; Arlete Santos and Mitch Blank at Archive Photos/Film; Holly Jones at AP/World Wide photos; Andy "Wild Turkey" McCord; my agent, Jim "the Bookworm" Hornfischer; my editor, James Robert Parish; my grammatical guru, Allan Taylor; and all the folks at Renaissance Books. Also, special thanks to Frank Smejkal for creating and maintaining the dumbest site on the Web: www.dumbest.com.

Thanks to the following for help with photos: John Anderson, The Texas State Library; Carolyn Bowler, Idaho State Historical Society; James B. Hill, John Fitzgerald Kennedy Library; Janis Olsen, Center for American History, The University of Texas; Mark Renovitch, Franklin D. Roosevelt Library; David J. Stanhope, Jimmy Carter Library.

Special thanks to Amelia, Diana, Joe, and Gene "Big Daddy of Border Radio" Fowler. Gene, you're the ram-what-am-with-every-lamb.

# CONTENTS

# THE THIRD-PARTY POLITICIANS

# INTRODUCTION

**Democrats do the dumbest things.** Just ask any Republican. And vice versa. "The more you read and observe about this politics thing," Will Rogers, the revered sage of Oklahoma, once noted, "you got to admit that each party is worse than the other."

Writer Ambrose Bierce defined politics as "the conduct of public affairs for private advantage." Perhaps it is too harsh to claim that every politician is corrupt. Napoleon Bonaparte was probably more accurate when he declared centuries ago, "In politics stupidity is not a handicap."

Stupidity, what an advantage! As Americans, we have come to expect politicians to do the dumbest things, and, generally, they have never let us down. For over two hundred years, we often have cast our votes for deadbeats, hypocrites, bigots, womanizers, drunks, and slobs, as well as good-hearted men and women who for some strange reason got into politics.

Are Democrats any dumber than Republicans? I believe this question should be answered by a vote. Check out what America thinks at our Web site (www.dumbest.com) and vote for yourself.

Are politicians less swift than other breeds of celebrities? As the co-author of *Movie Stars Do the Dumbest Things*, I have to agree with the celebrated actor Spencer Tracy who growled once, "Acting is not the noblest profession in the world, but there are things lower than acting—not many, mind you—but politicians give you something to look down on from time to time."

Compiling the present volume has been a humbling experience. "There is no credit to being a comedian when you have the whole government working for you," Will Rogers once admitted, "All you have to do is report the facts."

Indeed: Truth is dumber than fiction.

## KEY TO ENTRIES

I have restricted the entries in this book to politicians who have run for federal office (the U.S. House of Representatives, the U.S. Senate, or president of the United States), or for governor of a particular state. In the Local Loonies chapter, I have included some Democrats who ran for other state and local offices.

Politicians are identified as Pres. (President, if only the person's last name is cited), Rep. (Representative, if only the person's last name is used) for a member of the U.S. House of Representatives, Sen. (Senator, if only the person's last name is used) for a member of the U.S. Senate, or Gov. (Governor, if only the person's last name is used) for a state governor.

## DUMBEST QUOTE

Lists the dumbest quote or quotes spoken by the Democrat. When necessary for clarity, the quote is identified by year and/or circumstance.

## FACTS OF LIFE (and Death)

ORIGIN: Gives the full name, place of birth, date of birth, and (where appropriate) the date, place, and, if known, cause of death of the Democrat.

FORMATIVE YEARS: Lists the schools attended and the year of graduation.

FAMILY PLANNING: Lists spouses and dates of marriages and divorces of the Democrat. Note: This information is quite difficult to ascertain in several instances. For some reason, Democrats don't like talking about their ex-spouses.

SELECTED ELECTION SCORECARD: Includes major campaigns for president, the U.S. Senate, the U.S. House of Representatives, and state governor. Continuous elections to the same office are indicated by the year of first election to the year of last election (i.e., 1984–90). No distinction has been made between running for the presidency in a primary (to be chosen by the Democratic Party delegates as the candidate) or running in the general election. Note: The terms of federal office are as follows: U.S. House of Representatives, two years; U.S. Senate, six years; president, four years.

## QUICKIE BIO

A brief biography of the politician.

## ———— DOES THE DUMBEST THINGS

Lists the dumbest incidents in the career of the Democrat.


I have worked hard to provide the most accurate, up-to-date, and dumbest information available. All the anecdotes in this book have appeared previously in other publications. If you want more details, or you notice any errors, or if you know of some dumb stuff I have overlooked, please e-mail me at *politicians@dumbest.com*. Your nation (and my publisher) will thank you.

# THE
# DEMOCRATS

# Marion Barry

## FACTS OF LIFE

ORIGIN: Born Marion S. Barry Jr., March 6, 1936, Itta Bena, Mississippi.

FORMATIVE YEARS: LeMoyne College, B.S., 1958; Fisk University, M.A., 1960.

FAMILY PLANNING: Married Blantie C. Evans (student), 1962; divorced, 1969; married Mary Treadwell (phone company manager), 1973; divorced, 1976; married Effi Slaughter Cowell (teacher), 1977; divorced; married Cora Masters (Washington, D.C., employee), 1993.

SELECTED ELECTION SCORECARD: 1978–86: won, mayor, Washington, D.C. 1994: won, mayor, Washington, D.C.

## QUICKIE BIO

Described by his third wife as a naive "street dude," Marion Barry was born to a sharecropper family in Mississippi, earned a doctorate in chemistry, and taught at the University of Tennessee before he made the bad mistake of getting into politics. Young Professor Barry worked with Martin Luther King Jr., and moved to Washington, D.C., in 1965, where he was dubbed by the press a "dashiki-clad militant." Marion helped launch the "Free D.C." movement, which demanded that the black-majority district be given home rule. Barry got what he wanted and was elected mayor of a "free" D.C. in 1978. Unfortunately, Barry the chemist strongly believed in better living through chemistry, especially the illegal kind. He was busted for drugs in 1990 and served six months in prison. Miraculously he was reelected to the mayor's job, but wound up in rehab in 1996. In that same year, a Washington, D.C., official commented that Marion Barry was "a lot like nuclear power. On a good day, he can light the city. On a bad day, he can blow it up."

"B***h set me up!" Marion Barry exclaimed on videotape after he was caught smoking crack cocaine in an FBI sting.
(Courtesy of AP/World Wide Photos)

## MARION BARRY DOES
## THE DUMBEST THINGS

✪ Barry's middle initial *S* originally didn't stand for anything. In 1957, Marion took the middle name Shepilov in honor of a leader of the Soviet Communist Party.

✪ Barry was busted for allegedly writing bad checks in 1962.

✪ Police officers stopped Barry for jaywalking in 1967 and asked to see his ID. Marion shouted, "I ain't showing a white motherf***er a goddamn thing. . . . My name is nobody." When they tried to get Barry into the police wagon, Barry reportedly punched one of the cops in the face. When he was inside the wagon, he kicked the vehicle's door so hard it buckled. Barry was arrested for jaywalking, disorderly conduct, and destroying government property. He claimed it was all the fault of the police. Marion went to trial and was acquitted.

✪ Two years later, Barry confronted two police officers standing next to a vehicle that was parked illegally. "If you write a ticket on that car, I will kill you," Marion reportedly threatened. The law enforcer wrote the ticket, Barry ripped it up, and a fight ensued.

✪ Barry was arrested, and was released on bail. He arrived at the District Building, blamed the police for the incident, and announced, "We have declared war on the police department and this city. The police are like mad dogs." As Marion's supporters left the building, they broke glass bottles, tried to set the American flag on fire, shouted obscenities, punched a news vendor in the face, took flowers, and removed beer from a parked car.

✪ During Barry's term as mayor of the nation's capital, newspapers claimed that planes flew drugs from the Virgin Islands into D.C. and that some D.C. employees snorted cocaine at their office desks.

✪ In 1989, Marion made several visits to the Ramada Inn Central in Washington to the suite of Charles Lewis, a district employee and a native of the Virgin Islands. Traces of cocaine were later found in the room. At the Ramada, a man claimed that he came to talk with Barry about a job. Marion sat on the commode while the man spoke. Finally, the politician looked up and said, "You know, you look a lot like Santa Claus."

✪ During his third term as mayor, Barry remarked that the poor of D.C. were using the free ambulance system too often.

✪ After a welfare mother complained to Barry about the lack of housing for herself and her fourteen children, Marion advised her to "stop having all those babies."

✪ When hecklers booed Barry at a September 1989 neighborhood festival in Washington, he grinned and gave them the finger.

✪ In January 1987, a blizzard hit Washington, D.C. At the time, Marion Barry was in California watching the Washington Redskins play in the Super Bowl. When his city was unable to clear its streets of snow, Barry said that residents were exaggerating the situation, and delayed his return. He claimed that he had a hernia; others insisted that he had suffered a near fatal cocaine overdose.

✪ When Marion saw the cover of *Essence* magazine in 1977, he went gaga. He contacted the cover girl, Hazel Diane Rasheeda Moore and sought to persuade her to fly to D.C. She said no, and instead flew to London to visit her boyfriend. Oops! The day her plane landed in London, her beau was arrested for allegedly smuggling $18 million worth of heroin.

✪ Barry eventually got together with Rasheeda. Rasheeda claimed later that she had had sexual relations with Barry over one hundred times over three years at twenty-two different places, and had used marijuana, cocaine, crack, and opium with the mayor. She alleged that the mayor became paranoid when high. At one point, after smoking crack, he supposedly believed that the police were closing in on him, so he hid his crack-crystal drugs in a vacuum cleaner bag. When his paranoia subsided, Marion took the crystals from the bag, dusted them off, and smoked them.

★ At one point, Ms. Moore claimed, Barry took a massive hit of crack. When he exhaled his body started shaking and he almost collapsed. She grabbed the mayor and told him to stay focused. After regaining his composure, he looked at Moore and said, "That was a really good hit."

★ When Rasheeda tried to break up with Barry, he told her "Divine Providence" was behind their romance. He arranged for her to work on a summer youth program that received $180,000 worth of district funding. The name of the program? Project Me.

★ Allegedly, Barry threatened to cut off funding for Project Me after Rasheeda refused to have oral sex with him.

★ Rasheeda agreed to cooperate with the FBI on a sting operation. In January 1990, she invited the mayor to her room at Washington's Vista International Hotel. The videotape of the encounter revealed that Barry was more interested in sexual relations than drugs. He kept grabbing Rasheeda's breasts, and expressed his interest in having sex with multiple partners, "twos and threes if I can."

★ Eventually Barry smoked crack on camera, and was arrested immediately by the FBI. As they read him his rights, the mayor observed, repeatedly, on tape, "B***h set me up."

★ During Marion's trial, one witness stated that Barry liked to smoke cocaine-laced cigarettes that he called "M.B. specials." Barry was convicted on one count of drug possession.

★ After serving time, Marion was *reelected* mayor of Washington, D.C. However, the district was in such terrible shape that Congress stripped Mayor Barry of his power and the federal government once again took over control of D.C. Mayor Barry was left to supervise only a few agencies, including the Office of Cable TV and the Department of Recreation.

# Jerry Brown

## FACTS OF LIFE

ORiGiN: Born Edmund Gerald "Jerry" Brown Jr., April 7, 1938, San Francisco, California.

FORMATiVE YEARS: Los Gatos Novitiate (a Jesuit Seminary) 1956–1960, then dropped out; University of California at Berkeley, B.A., 1961; Yale Law School, J.D., 1964.

FAMiLY PLANNiNG: Unmarried.

SELECTED ELECTiON SCORECARD: 1974: won, governor, California. 1976: lost, U.S. president. 1978: won, governor, California. 1980: lost, U.S. president. 1982: lost, U.S. Senate, California. 1992: lost, U.S. president. 1998: won, mayor, Oakland, California.

## QUICKIE BIO

Protect the Earth, Serve the People, and Explore the Universe." "Wow, what a far-out campaign slogan!" Yeah, man, Jerry Brown used it when he ran for president in 1980. "Jerry Brown? Who was Jerry Brown?" You know, man, Jerry Brown, the political dude who hung out with Catholic monks, then studied law, failed the state bar, hung out with Mother Teresa, practiced Zen, got into state politics, and became the governor of California, just like his father. "Whoa, dude—governor?" Yeah, Governor Moonbeam. He spent time

19

with space visionaries, solar-power advocates, a fast-food franchise pioneer, a former Green Beret, and singer Linda Ronstadt. He even ran for president several times and lost. "I remember, dude! His press secretary once rapped, 'Jerry's big problem is that he's thinking forty years in the future. He's out on Uranus half the time.' " Guess what, dude, he came back from Uranus and won the election as mayor of Oakland. Mayor Jerry said that he wanted to turn Oakland into "an ecopolis, like an Italian hill town." Can you dig it, man? "Yeah, Oakland's full of hills." Yeah, man. And so's Uranus.

## JERRY BROWN DOES
## THE DUMBEST THINGS

✪ Jerry Brown's life was changed after his friend, filmmaker Jacques Barzaghi, took him to a Zen Buddhist center in California. Barzaghi had four mandalas tattooed on his body, exclaiming to a reporter, "I'm not sure why I have them."

✪ Governor Brown liked to walk up and down the halls of the California state capitol building, bouncing a rubber ball up and down on a wooden paddle.

✪ Governor Jerry made a state visit to Japan in 1976. On the flight, a magazine article caught his interest. "What about this place China?" Jerry asked. "Why don't we go to China?"

✪ Governor Brown left a reception at the American Embassy in Tokyo to attend the Rolling Coconut Revue, a concert by American rock stars to save the whales. "The whales," Brown reflected, "it's a problem. What are we going to save, and what are we not going to save?"

✪ Governor Brown, a self-described "senior space cadet," convened California Space Day in August 1977, and declared, "I don't think the frontier is closed. It's just opening up in space. That opening up, that exploration, is first and foremost a discovery of the unknown, a breaking out of the egocentric, man-dominated perceptions that still tie us down here below." After Jerry's speech, famed undersea explorer and TV personality Jacques Cousteau jumped up and shouted, "We've got to go all the way in all directions."

✪ According to a top aide, Jerry got friendly with an attractive young woman in Jackson, California. The two retired upstairs. Later that night, the guests awakened to slamming doors and loud shouts. As it turned out, the woman was furious with the governor because he had gulped down a glass of water, and her contact lenses had been in the water.

★ When he ran for president in 1976, Jerry was driven around in a 1974 Plymouth Satellite and referred to himself as the "uncandidate." His campaign produced buttons which had no words on them, just the color brown.

★ When asked why he supported Brown, actor Warren Beatty observed, "In the long run what you're looking for in a politician is someone who's . . . you know . . . someone who's in the middle of his body."

★ Arriving at a campaign stop during the 1976 primary in Las Vegas, Brown looked around and asked, "Where's the center of this experience?" Then he answered his own question. "The center is wherever you are. It's internal. Let's have a cup of coffee."

★ In 1980, during the Wisconsin primary, filmmaker Francis Ford Coppola produced a half-hour television program for Presidential Candidate Jerry, to be broadcast live from the state capital using a $500,000 Swiss projection system. Rock promoter Bill Graham warmed up the crowd with jokes like, "Coke is bad for your sex life." Then the projection system screwed up. As the candidate appeared on-screen, electronic worms burrowed across his face, and he said, "I wanted to find out what was inside me. I wanted to find God. I really didn't want politics." Brown's spacey broadcast preempted a popular Easter program featuring Peter Cottontail. Thousands of kids were furious at Jerry for taking away their rabbit. Jerry quit the campaign soon after.

★ During his 1998 campaign for mayor of Oakland, Brown talked about the danger of greenhouse gases. When he won the election, a band called the Naked Barbies played at his victory party. One of his opponents sighed, "This has been like running against Elvis."

" At least when I was governor, cocaine was expensive," bragged Jerry Brown, here shown during his unsuccessful 1992 bid for the Democratic Presidential Nomination.
(Courtesy of AP/World Wide Photos)

# Jimmy Carter

## All-American Presidential Bonus Chapter

### FACTS OF LIFE

ORIGIN: Born James "Jimmy" Earl Carter Jr., October 1, 1924, Plains, Georgia.

FORMATIVE YEARS: U.S. Naval Academy, B.S., 1946.

FAMILY PLANNING: Married Eleanor Rosalynn Smith (student), July 7, 1946.

SELECTED ELECTION SCORECARD: 1966: lost, governor, Georgia. 1970: won, governor, Georgia. 1976: won, U.S. president. 1980: lost, U.S. president.

### QUICKIE BIO

You show me a good loser and I will show you a loser," declared Jimmy Carter in 1966. Jimmy Carter became one of the biggest losers in the history of presidential politics. A born-again Christian who worked in the Navy nuclear submarine program, Carter went back home to Georgia to operate the family peanut farm. He served on his local school board for seven years, then as governor of Georgia before winning election as U.S. president in a closely fought election against Pres. Gerald Ford. President Carter eschewed the trappings of his federal office as he sought to lead the nation down a narrow moral path. Americans claimed they wanted a good man to be president, but Carter was just too good—and he also had a terrible run of bad political luck. During his administration, the Three Mile Island nuclear plant near Harrisburg, Pennsylvania, was threatened with a possible meltdown, the United States wallowed in recession, and Iranian militants stormed the U.S. Embassy in Tehran, taking sixty-six American hostages. At the end of his term, Carter had the lowest approval rating ever recorded for an American president, even lower than Nixon's rating right before he resigned from the White House. After getting thrashed by Ronald Reagan in the 1980 election, Carter moved on to a career building houses for the needy and participating in elections all over the world—this time as an observer, not a candidate.

## JIMMY CARTER DOES THE DUMBEST THINGS

★ Carter claimed to be a "nuclear physicist," but wasn't.

★ As a kid, Jimmy took his mother's diamond engagement ring to school, gave it to his teacher, and told her, "My daddy can always buy Mama another one."

★ A year before he was elected governor of Georgia, Carter attended a Lions Club meeting early one morning and saw a light in the sky. The candidate filed a UFO sighting report and wrote that it appeared "bluish at first—then reddish—but not solid. . . ." The peanut-farming politician then declared, "I'll never make fun of people who say they've seen unidentified objects in the sky."

★ A few weeks after he moved into the Georgia governor's mansion, Carter decided to build a tennis court and a swimming pool there. He explained his decision by saying, "I can think better at the bottom of a swimming pool that I can at some other places."

★ After being elected governor, Carter arrived at a small town in southwest Georgia. He went into a restaurant and ordered hotcakes. After being served his food, Carter asked the waitress for butter. She said no. Carter asked again. Again the waitress said no. The next time the waitress came around Jimmy grumped, "Listen, I don't want to make an issue of this, but I want some more butter." She said, "You're not going to have it." He responded, "Do you know who I am?" She asked, "Who?" He answered, "I'm the governor of Georgia." The server retorted, "Do you know who I am?" "No," Carter replied. The waitress proclaimed, "I'm the keeper of the butter."

Jimmy Carter, who described himself as a "nuclear physicist" and a "lover of Bob Dylan's songs," invited Willie Nelson and Emmy Lou Harris to perform at the White House. Willie later went up on the roof of the president's pad and smoked a joint.
(Courtesy of Jimmy Carter Library)

⭐ While he was governor, Carter was at the airport by 7:00 A.M. one day. His plane began to taxi down the runway when he saw his traveling companion running to meet the plane. Jimmy ordered the pilot to take off, and snapped, "If he can't be here on time, it's too bad."

⭐ When Jimmy informed his mother he was going to run for president, she inquired, "President of what?"

⭐ When he began his bid for president, Carter said that he would not lie and told interviewers, "I don't think I would ever take on the same frame of mind that [Richard] Nixon and [Lyndon] Johnson did, lying, cheating, and distorting the truth." He later apologized to Johnson's wife, Lady Bird.

⭐ Presidential candidate Carter did an interview with *Playboy* magazine in 1976. In the Q & A session he admitted that he had committed adultery in his heart, and paraphrased Jesus Christ as saying, "Don't consider yourself better than someone else because one guy screws a whole bunch of women while the other guy is loyal to his wife." After the *Playboy* interview, bumper stickers appeared with the slogan, "In his heart he knows your wife."

- Campaigning for president in Mississippi, Carter visited a department store and shook a bunch of hands, including that of a mannequin. Jimmy told his aide, "Better give her a brochure too."

- When asked in 1976 about the big age difference between his three grown sons and his youngest daughter Amy, Carter explained, "My wife and I had an argument for fourteen years . . . which I finally won."

- President Carter definitely committed lust in his heart when he had dinner with actress Elizabeth Taylor. Seated across the table from the voluptuous superstar, Jimmy couldn't look away from her. She returned his glance and asked him a question. He continued to stare, ignoring her question. "Well, Mr. Carter?" Liz purred. "I'm sorry Ms. Taylor," the president admitted nervously. "I'm sure you were talking to me but I didn't hear a word that you said."

- When asked how he would feel if his daughter told him she had had an affair, Carter replied that he would be "shocked and overwhelmed," especially because his girl was "only seven years old."

- Carter did let himself walk on the wild side a little bit. For example, in 1976 he attended a party in Beverly Hills hosted by swinger and movie star Warren Beatty. "It is a thrill to meet the famous people here tonight," said the born-again political candidate. "I hope I don't get to know too much about you."

- Jimmy was always painfully earnest. On the campaign trail in 1976, he was asked about growing peanuts and waxed eloquently, "I think that the image of a peanut . . . being kind of small and insignificant, but cumulatively being very important to the American people, is one that fairly accurately mirrors the kind of campaign that we've run."

- "Jimmy sure bit off a hunk this time," Billy Carter said when he heard that his brother was running for U.S. president, "but he just might do it." When he did win, Billy tried to capitalize on his sibling's name by launching Billy Beer. Billy Carter went to New York to promote his product. According to New York's Mayor Ed Koch, Billy was a "wacko" who was "drunk all day long." At one point, bleary-eyed Billy asked Koch, "You want me to endorse you? What are you, a Republican or a Democrat?"

- Billy also promoted the Vancouver World Belly Flop and Cannonball Diving Contest in British Columbia, Canada. It flopped.

- President Carter knew about his sibling's limitations. "I've tried to involve Billy in the government," he admitted once. "I was going to put the CIA and the FBI together, but Billy said he wouldn't head an agency that he couldn't spell."

★ "Jimmy's still mad because I wouldn't take secretary of state," Billy countered. "I want to be director of alcohol and firearms."

★ The chief executive's brother managed to concoct an even dumber idea. In 1980, with Jimmy running for reelection as president, and American hostages being held by Islamic fundamentalists in Iran, Billy Carter registered as an agent of the Libyan government. He revealed that he had been given $220,000 in what he called "loans" from Libya. The Justice Department and the U.S. Senate investigated. It developed that Billy had begun working for the Libyans in 1978. Billy traveled to Libya twice, and on one trip he sat in seats reserved for the PLO (Palestine Liberation Organization), and sat right next to one of their most important arms suppliers. Billy defended himself by saying, "There's a helluva lot more Arabians than there is Jews." When Jews objected, Billy spewed, "Jewish critics can kiss my a**."

★ Rosalynn Carter suggested that her brother-in-law Billy use his friendship with Libya to gain release of the hostages in Iran. Billy hosted his Libyan buddies on a visit to the U.S. While he waited for their plane to land, brother Billy peed on the tarmac.

★ President Carter had problems with a bad interpreter in Poland. When Jimmy said the he had "left the United States," the translator made him sound as if he had "abandoned the United States." When the American visitor referred to Poland's "desires for the future," the audience heard about Poland's "lusts for the future." The interpreter also told the audience, "The president says he is pleased to be here in Poland grasping your private parts."

★ Carter didn't get along well with the media. "I'm not going to say anything terribly important tonight," he told a gathering of reporters, "so you can all put away your crayons."

★ Jimmy became a born-again Christian in 1966, and did missionary work in the Northeast. He even did some as president; in 1979, he met with the president of South Korea, who was a Buddhist, and tried to convert him to Christianity.

★ A black supporter complained about the president's "Jesus bit." "He'd cup my face with his hand, ever so gently, like he was the Messiah," the man insisted. "It drives me crazy."

✪ Jimmy did not approve of all Christians. "In a very Christian way," he said, concerning the Rev. Jerry Falwell, "as far as I'm concerned, he can go to hell."

✪ As his administration began to fall apart in 1979, a reporter asked Carter if his daughter Amy bragged about her daddy being president. "No," Carter sighed. "She probably apologizes."

✪ In 1979, Jimmy Carter described the Shah of Iran as "an island of stability." A few months later, the royal ruler was deposed by the Ayatollah Khomeini. Shortly thereafter, Iranian students stormed the U.S. Embassy in Tehran and began the hostage crisis.

✪ Perhaps President Carter's dumbest move while in the Oval Office was to dispatch a rescue squad to free the American prisoners held in Iran. The "mission impossible" took place in April 1980. At a staging site in the Iranian desert, a sandstorm blew in and an American helicopter collided with a transport plane, killing eight soldiers and wounding five others. The mission was aborted, and the captives remained hostages until Ronald Reagan's presidential inauguration day in January 1981.

✪ At the 1980 Democratic Convention, when introducing Sen. Hubert Humphrey (D-Minnesota), Jimmy Carter declared, "I am speaking of a great man who should have been president and would have been one of the greatest presidents in history—Hubert Horatio Hornblower."

✪ During his reelection campaign in 1980, Carter tried to relax by going fishing in a canoe on a small lake near his home in Plains, Georgia. Horrors! A bunny jumped into the lake, hissing and baring its teeth as it made its way toward the chief executive. Carter took the canoe paddle and slapped the water in front of the rabbit. The press dubbed the critter "killer rabbit" and "Bonzai bunny." One wit quipped, "I'm sure the rabbit intended the president no harm. In fact, the poor thing was simply doing something a little unusual these days—trying to get aboard the president's boat. Everyone else seems to be jumping ship." Carter lost the election.

# Bill Clinton

## All-American Presidential Bonus Chapter

### FACTS OF LIFE

ORIGIN: Born William Jefferson Blythe IV, August 19, 1946, Hope, Arkansas. (Legally changed his surname in 1967 to match that of his stepfather.)

FORMATIVE YEARS: Georgetown University, B.S., 1968; Rhodes Scholar, Oxford University, 1968–70; Yale Law School, J.D., 1973.

FAMILY PLANNING: Married Hillary Rodham (lawyer), October 11, 1975.

SELECTED ELECTION SCORECARD: 1974: lost, U.S. House of Representatives, 3rd District, Arkansas. 1978: won, governor, Arkansas. 1980: lost, governor, Arkansas. 1982–90: won, governor, Arkansas. 1992–96: won, U.S. president.

# QUICKIE BIO

"My doctor ordered me to shut up," a laryngitis-stricken Bill Clinton rasped, "which will make every American happy!" Yes! After several years of Clinton in the White House, America was ready for the sax-playing, sexually voracious president to shut up.

Clinton was a native of Hope, Arkansas, but the circumstances of his birth were almost hopeless. He was born out-of-wedlock. Some say that his alleged father wasn't really his dad—who, in any event, was already married to someone else when he wed Clinton's mother, and died a few months before Bill's birth. After Clinton's mother remarried, Bill reportedly had to stop his alcoholic stepdad from beating her. Despite, or maybe because of, the turmoil at home, the boy became an overachieving student, who ran for so many elections in high school he was nicknamed "Vote Clinton" and was banned there from further campaigning. He went on to Oxford University in England (as a prestigious Rhodes scholar) and Yale Law School in Connecticut where he met his future wife, Hillary Rodham, in the library.

As governor of Arkansas, Clinton was known as "the Boy Wonder." As president of the United States, he became "Slick Willie." Republicans accused Clinton of unethical behavior during his first term, and the Office of the Independent Council under Ken Starr began an investigation of the so-called Whitewater real-estate scandal. At the same time, Clinton was sued by Arkansas receptionist Paula Jones for sexual harassment (which allegedly occurred when he was governor). The Whitewater investigation changed into an examination of President Clinton's sex life, which led to the impeachment and trial of him as president in 1999. Like Pres. Andrew Johnson (D-Tennessee) in the 1860s, Clinton was cleared of all charges, although Bill was later fined for lying in the sexual harassment case. As the nation suffered from "Clinton fatigue," a White House press secretary announced, "We may do dumb things from time to time, but we are not certifiably insane." And how much did Starr spend on his futile investigation of Clinton before retiring from the Independent Counsel Office in October 1999? $47 million. Now *that's* dumb.

## BILL CLINTON DOES
## THE DUMBEST THINGS

⭐ In 1963, when he was seventeen, Bill Clinton traveled to Washington, D.C., where he met and shook hands with Pres. John F. Kennedy. After the introduction, Clinton decided to be just like Kennedy. He succeeded.

⭐ What was it about JFK that most amazed Clinton? According to Clinton's White House aide George Stephanopoulos, President Clinton was agog that Kennedy's cortisone treatments for Addison's disease super-charged his sex drive.

✪ Young Bill Clinton liked to cruise around in an El Camino pickup truck, and recalled, "It was a real sort of Southern deal. I had Astroturf in the back. You don't want to know why, but I did." Clinton confessed later, "I'm someone who has a deep emotional attachment to *Starsky and Hutch.*"

✪ "When I was in England," presidential candidate Clinton told reporters in March 1992, "I experimented with marijuana a time or two and I didn't like it, and I didn't inhale, and I never tried it again." Maybe not, but according to others, Clinton reportedly smoked pot while he was run-ning Sen. George McGovern's (D-South Dakota) 1972 presidential cam-paign in Texas. He also allegedly smoked pot in the Arkansas state capitol building.

✪ Clinton's stepbrother Roger was ten years younger and, supposedly, a lot druggier. In 1984, Roger told undercover cops on a surveillance tape: "Got to get some for my brother; he's got a nose like a vacuum cleaner." Roger later served prison time on cocaine charges.

✪ In 1990, a former bartender at the club where Roger played in a rock band told a federal grand jury that, one night, she supplied Governor Clinton with cocaine. Soon after testifying, the woman was arrested and sentenced to thirty-one years in prison for selling half an ounce of pot and $100 worth of amphetamines. Her conviction was later reversed.

✪ The manager of Roger Clinton's apartment complex in Little Rock, Arkansas, had an office next to Roger's pad, and claimed that she could hear Roger talking with Bill Clinton about the pot they smoked and the coke they sniffed. The manager and her husband kept notes on the conversations, which were stolen from their office in 1993. Two months later, the manager's husband was killed in a Little Rock suburb.

✪ Bill was introduced as the smartest of the candidates seeking the Democratic presidential nomination at a New Hampshire campaign appearance in 1991. He responded, "Isn't that a little like calling Moe the most intelligent of the Three Stooges?"

✪ In 1993, Clinton tied up air traffic at the Los Angeles airport so that he could get a $200 haircut in the presidential jet. Sen. Bob Dole (R-Kansas) dubbed the plane *"Hair Force One."*

✪ Many of the accusations against Bill came from Arkansas state troopers who served as his bodyguards while he was governor of Arkansas. Not

"I don't care if he boned a sheep, if that's his thing," Whoopi Goldberg said about her buddy President Bill Clinton. Clinton didn't bone Whoopi, but he did invite Barbra Streisand for a sleepover in the White House while First Lady Hillary was in Arkansas with her dying father.
(Courtesy of Reuters/Mike Theiler/Archive Photos)

only was Bill foolish enough to act up in front of the troopers, but many of the state troopers were Republicans.

★ Clinton was a man of big appetites. "When he would eat an apple," explained an Arkansas state trooper, "he would eat the whole thing, core, stem, and seeds. He would pick up a baked potato with his hands and eat it in two bites. I've never seen anything like it."

★ One state trooper explained that Governor Clinton liked to scope out women who he described as having a "come-hither look." Then he would send a trooper to inquire whether the woman was interested in meeting Clinton. If she was game, the trooper reportedly would bring her to Clinton, who was usually waiting in a private area. The troopers claimed that Governor Clinton had about six "steady girlfriends whom he saw two or three times a week."

★ When one trooper asked Clinton to sign an autograph for a female friend, the governor asked, "Does she have big titties?"

★ So many bimbos, so little time. Clinton was involved in numerous scandals, including Whitewater, Filegate, and Travelgate. But by far the dumbest things Clinton did involved women. One of Clinton's aides began keeping lists of Bill's girlfriends in 1988, and counted a total of twenty-six women who might cause problems if he got into national politics. After Clinton moved up into national politics, many of the women on the list did indeed cause him problems. His assistants referred to these situations as "bimbo eruptions."

✪ Several of the "bimbo eruptions" occurred during the Paula Jones trial in which Clinton was accused of sexual harassment. Jones's attorneys interviewed other women about Clinton's sex life, to prove a pattern of such harassment. The testimony of these women, known as "Jane Does," caught the eyes of Ken Starr and the Office of the Independent Council. Starr had begun investigating Clinton's involvement with the Whitewater real-estate shenanigans in Arkansas, in August 1994. In January 1998 Starr was allowed to expand his investigation to include an examination of the Monica Lewinsky material submitted for the Paula Jones trial, which, later, formed the basis of the charges for which Clinton was impeached and tried by the House of Representatives. Reporters uncovered the identities of most of the Jane Does, including Monica Lewinsky. In addition to the Jane Does, other women came forward with their own Clinton stories. Taken as a whole, the accounts of Bill's bimbos establish a pattern of the dumbest sexual behavior ever demonstrated by any president. Except maybe JFK. Or LBJ. . . . Or FDR. . . . Or Warren Harding. Or . . .

### BILL CLINTON DOES THE DUMBEST THINGS (ALLEGEDLY) WITH BIMBOS

## JUANITA BRODERICK

✪ Juanita (a campaign worker) claimed that Clinton came to her hotel room for a visit while she was working on his first gubernatorial campaign. A few minutes after she arrived, he reportedly started kissing her, pulled her onto the bed, and, supposedly, forced her to have sex. During the alleged rape, Juanita claimed that Clinton grabbed her upper lip with his mouth, and bruised it. "The last thing he said to me," she told the press, "was, 'You better get some ice for that.' And he put on his sunglasses and walked out the door."

✪ Thirteen years later, Clinton met Juanita again in Little Rock. "It was unreal," Juanita said. "He kept trying to hold my hand. I can still remember his words. He said, 'Can you ever forgive me? I'm not the same man I used to be. . . .' I told him, 'You just go to hell.' "

## DOLLY KYLE BROWNING

⭐ Dolly (a high-school sweetheart) claimed that she had an affair with Clinton that began when they were teens and continued until 1992. "I resent being lumped into that bunch of other women!" Browning declared to writers who included her on Clinton's bimbo list: "This is the one relationship Billy has never denied—never!"

⭐ Dolly alleged that in May 1988 she spent the night in a Dallas hotel with the future president and told him that she had been attending meetings of a Sex Addicts Anonymous support group. When she asked, "Did you ever think you were a sex addict?" Bill answered, "I know I am, and I've tried to overcome it. But it's so hard. Women are everywhere, and for some reason they seem to want me."

⭐ When the tabloids approached Dolly in 1992 and expressed interest in reporting her story, Browning called Bill to ask his advice. He refused to talk to Dolly and supposedly sent her brother to threaten her if she went to the press. In 1994 Dolly and Bill met at their thirtieth high-school reunion in Hot Springs, Arkansas. Clinton approached her, acting like nothing ever had happened. When the president said, "How are you?" She responded reportedly, "You are such an a**hole. I can't believe you'd even bother to ask." The two talked for over an hour at the side of the auditorium. Dolly later wrote a novel (*Purposes of the Heart*, 1995) about their alleged love affair.

## BETH GLADDEN COULSON

⭐ Beth (a judge) was the wife of one of Clinton's biggest campaign contributors. Clinton later appointed her to serve on the Arkansas Court of Appeals. He denied ever having sex with her, although Arkansas state troopers claimed that they drove Clinton to her house on a number of occasions when her husband was not there, and waited for Bill in the driveway. One such law enforcer recalled going to the Little Rock airport to pick up the governor. When he arrived, Clinton told the state trooper that he would drive in Beth's Jaguar. According to the man, "On the ride back, he drove, and she was nowhere to be seen in the car."

⭐ After the vehicular incident, Clinton told the trooper that the only sex he indulged in was oral sex. Clinton explained that he had researched sex in the Bible and found that oral sex wasn't considered adultery. Bill also said that oral sex was the safest type, because stomach acids would act on swallowed semen to kill any possible AIDS virus. But even if it were considered adultery, Clinton was ready for that. According to another trooper, Clinton gave him one of the books he had used in 1973 to prepare for his Arkansas bar exam: "There's a sentence . . . to the effect that 'Adultery is not a crime' that is underlined twice in red."

## Gennifer Flowers

✪ In 1997, during his deposition for the Paula Jones trial, Clinton admitted that he had had sex with Gennifer Flowers (a reporter), but only once. Gennifer, on the other hand, claimed that she had an affair with the president for twelve years, and blabbed, "We made love everywhere, on the floor, in bed, in the kitchen, on the cabinet, the sink . . . "

✪ Gennifer claimed that Bill called her "Pookie," and that she called him "Baby" or "Darling." She nicknamed her vagina "Precious," and Bill supposedly nicknamed his penis "Willard" or "Willy." She further detailed, "I called his testicles 'the boys' and he called my breasts 'the girls.' " When they talked on the phone Flowers would know that Bill was not alone if he started the conversation by asking, "How are the girls?"

✪ A state trooper, who, supposedly had had an affair with Gennifer himself, claimed that Clinton bragged that Flowers "could suck a tennis ball through a garden hose."

✪ Gennifer suggested that the president was eager to please although he was "not particularly well endowed." Clinton once left his T-shirt behind so that Gennifer could have his scent nearby. She claimed that Bill tried to convince her to have sex with him inside the men's room of the Arkansas governor's mansion.

✪ Flowers recalled that Clinton dripped honey and melted ice on her naked body, and that she spanked him. She also alleged that they smoked pot together, and she asserted, "He did inhale."

✪ Gennifer taped many of her telephone conversations with the president, which she later sold as "the love tapes."

## Elizabeth Ward Gracen

✪ Elizabeth (an actress) was crowned Miss America in 1981 and acted in the TV series *Highlander: The Raven*. She claimed that she met Clinton in 1983 in Arkansas while filming public-service announcements. Clinton flirted with her in his limo and then they had sex several days later at a Little Rock apartment. Nine years later, her agent supposedly met with two of Clinton's friends and worked out an agreement for her to deny any hanky-panky with Bill. After making the pact, she said, she had a much easier time getting acting jobs. Five years later still, she fled the country to avoid testifying in the Paula Jones court case.

## CONNIE HAMZY

✪ Connie, a self-described "rock groupie" who was immortalized in the 1973 Grand Funk Railroad hit "We're an American Band," claimed that she was lounging by the pool of a Little Rock, Arkansas, hotel, when a friend came by and said that Governor Clinton wanted to meet her. "We ended up in an alcove making out like crazy," Connie recalled later. "He was kissing me, and his hands were all over me." When others insisted that she pulled down her top and tried to seduce the governor, she replied, "That's ridiculous. . . . I'm a rock groupie. Politicians are not my thing." After passing lie-detector tests about her story, Connie said, "I may be a slut, but I'm not a lying slut."

## MARILYN JO JENKINS

✪ Marilyn (an office worker) worked for a Little Rock power company that donated money to the 1996 Clinton presidential reelection campaign. Bill admitted that he met Marilyn at her apartment at least ten times. One state trooper led Marilyn into the Arkansas governor's mansion at 5:15 A.M. through a basement door and stood watch at the basement entrance to keep an eye out for Hillary. Phone records reflect that Clinton made fifty-nine phone calls to Marilyn from 1989 to 1991, including a ninety-four-minute call from a hotel room that began at 1:23 A.M.

✪ State troopers assigned to Clinton maintained that Marilyn picked Clinton up in her car when he was jogging, and dropped him off later on his jogging route. When Clinton returned to the mansion, he used the troopers' bathroom to splash water on his face to look like he had been sweating.

## PAULA CORBIN JONES

✪ In February 1994, Paula (a receptionist) accused Clinton of sexually harassing her nearly three years earlier. According to her complaint, Jones was working as a receptionist at a Little Rock hotel when a state trooper handed her a slip of paper with a room number, and said, "The governor would like to meet with you." The trooper told Jones, "It is okay, we do this all the time for the governor." Paula went to the room. After a few minutes Governor Bill reportedly asked, "Are you married?" When Paula said that she had a regular boyfriend, Clinton reportedly pulled his pants down, exposing his erect penis, and, supposedly, said,

"Kiss it." Paula said, "Look, I've got to go," and left. Clinton was at the hotel that day for a Governor's Quality Management Conference.

✪ Paula asserted she could prove her story because "there were distinguishing characteristics in Clinton's genital area." The particulars were reported to be Peyronie's syndrome, which is a distinct angular bend or curvature of the penis. The issue did not play a significant part in the Jones-Clinton trial.

✪ Jones filed a lawsuit against Clinton in May 1994. Clinton's lawyers tried to have the case postponed until after he was out of office. In January 1996, a federal appeals court ruled that the case could go forward. A year later, it was presented before the U.S. Supreme Court. Six men in trench coats, boots, and boxer shorts carried a sign outside that read "Flashers Support Clinton." In May 1997 the court ruled in Jones's favor and the trial continued. It ended in July 1999, when Clinton was ordered to pay Jones more than $90,000, the first time a sitting American president had ever been fined for contempt of court.

## Sheila Lawrence

✪ Sheila, a socialite and the widow of a major Democratic Party contributor, denied rumors of a 1992 affair with the president. However, after her husband's death in 1996 (he was thirty-five years older than she), Sheila used her political influence to have him buried in Arlington National Cemetery, claiming that he had been wounded in World War II and had been given a medal by the Russians. Her spouse was interred at Arlington, then exhumed and moved when no military service records or medal could be found.

## Monica Lewinsky

✪ "I want to say one thing to the American people. I want you to listen to me," President Clinton declared on January 26, 1998. "I'm going to say this again: I did not have sexual relations with that woman, Miss Lewinsky [an intern]." Eight months later, President Clinton hung his head in shame and admitted, "I did have a relationship with Miss Lewinsky that was not appropriate. In fact, it was wrong." He added, "I don't think there is a fancy way to say that I have sinned." But notice, he did not say he had sexual relations with "that woman." What he did have was, perhaps, the dumbest relationship in the history of American politics. Actually, the "relationship" turned out to be a three-way between Bill Clinton, investigator Kenneth Starr, and Monica Lewinsky. The sordid tale began in June 1995 when twenty-one-year-old Monica went to work at the White House as a unpaid intern. Monica claimed she had her first sexual encounter with President Clinton in November 1995. Eleven days later she was on the payroll, and worked at the White House until she was transferred to the Pentagon in April 1996. Lewinsky asserted that she continued to see the president while she was employed at the Pentagon. Monica first revealed her story in depositions taken for the Paula Jones legal case against Clinton. In his deposition for the Paula Jones suit, Clinton denied having "sexual relations" with Lewinsky, which, according to the definition presented by government investigator Ken Starr would have required Clinton to have touched Monica's "genitalia, anus, groin, breast, inner thigh or buttocks" in order to "arouse or gratify" her sexually. The perjury charge against Clinton brought by the House of Representatives which resulted in his impeachment and trial revolved mainly around the question of whether or not Clinton had had sex with Monica and then lied about it on the record.

★ In August 1998, Clinton appeared before a grand jury called by Starr (a prosecutor) to investigate Clinton's relationship with Monica Lewinsky. When asked about his attorney's assertion during the deposition for the Paula Jones case that "there is absolutely no sex of any kind" between the chief executive and Monica Lewinsky, the president testified, "It depends on what the meaning of the word 'is' is." Other Clinton gems before Ken Starr's grand jury included: "I have not had sex with her [Monica] as I defined it," and, "There were a lot of times when we were alone, but I never thought we were." During his trial on the floor of the House of Representatives, Clinton's lawyer claimed that the president committed "interpretations of contorted definitions," not perjury.

★ To prove perjury, Ken Starr catalogued Clinton's sexual activity with Monica in the Starr report: "According to Monica, she claimed to have performed oral sex on the president on nine occasions. Monica said, 'There was no penetration.' On all nine of those occasions, the president fondled and kissed her bare breasts. He touched her genitals, both through her underwear and directly, bringing her to orgasm on two occasions. On one occasion, the president inserted a cigar into her vagina. On another occasion, she and the president had brief genital-to-genital contact." Starr reported that after Clinton inserted the cigar into Monica's vagina in March 1996, he withdrew it, "put the cigar in his mouth and said to Ms. Lewinsky, 'It tastes good.' "

★ A week after the infamous cigar incident, on Easter Sunday, Clinton invited Monica to the White House. While Bill was enjoying Lewinsky's company, his advisor Dick Morris phoned. Clinton took the call while Monica supposedly kept busy.

✪ After the Easter Sunday encounter, Lewinsky claimed, Clinton promised her a job if he won the reelection. "You can do anything you want," Bill told her, according to the Starr Report. "You can be anything you want." When Monica purportedly asked, "Well, can I be Assistant to the President for Blow Jobs?" the president said, "I'd like that."

✪ In December 1997, Monica went to President Clinton's office carrying gifts which included a silver cigar holder, a mug, and a tie. According to the Starr Report, she stormed out when she learned that Clinton was busy in his office with leggy TV personality Eleanor Mondale, the daughter of former Vice President Walter Mondale. The president soothed Monica's jealous rage by saying, "Do you think I'm stupid enough to go running with someone I'm messing around with?"

✪ Starr also noted in his investigation that Monica and Bill had phone sex seventeen times. In every case, Bill was the instigator. Monica claimed that the president called her at 6:30 A.M. on the day he left to visit the Olympic Games in Atlanta. Afterwards, according to the Starr report, "the president exclaimed, 'Good morning!' and then said: 'What a way to start a day.' "

✪ Per the Starr Report, Monica showed the president an e-mail describing the effects of chewing Altoids before performing oral sex. Although she was chewing Altoids at the time, the chief executive said he didn't have time for oral sex because he was going to a state dinner for the president of Mexico.

✪ In January 1998, Monica's friend Linda Tripp turned over to Ken Starr tapes she had made of her own telephone conversations with Lewinsky. When talking to Tripp, Monica referred to Clinton as "the creep" because all he wanted was oral sex.

✪ In January 1998, the news media broke the story that Lewinsky claimed she was saving a navy-blue dress as a souvenir because it was stained with presidential semen. Monica said later, "I was going to clean it. I was going to wear it again." She confessed that, "It [the stain] could have been spinach dip or something."

✪ Once the scandal broke, Monica Lewinsky became a celebrity of the moment. She wrote a bestseller (Monica's Book, 1999), and marketed a line of handbags. She said she took up sewing while she was living in Washington, forbidden by prosecutors to contact anyone. She later became a spokesperson for a weight loss company.

✪ Monica's stepfather received a fund-raising letter from the Clinton Legal Expense Trust, asking him for a donation. He wrote on the envelope, "Return to sender. You must be morons to send me this letter."

# SALLY PERDUE

⭐ Sally Perdue (a reporter) claimed on TV that she had a four-month fling with Bill Clinton in 1983. An Arkansas state trooper stated that he often drove Clinton to Sally's home, and waited while Clinton entertained the young woman. Bill often brought his saxophone to play for Sally, and supposedly once played it for her with her negligee over his head. Perdue alleged that Clinton smoked pot with her, saying it "enhanced his sexual pleasure." According to Sally, Bill offered her marijuana and cocaine during his visits: "He had all the equipment lined out, like a real pro." When Clinton got ready to go, he flicked the patio light on and off to summon the trooper.

# MARSHA SCOTT

⭐ Marsha (an office worker) bragged to her boyfriend, "I've had sex with Bill Clinton every Christmas for thirty years, ever since we were in our early twenties in Arkansas. It's my annual Christmas present to him!" Marsha refused to talk to the press.

# KATHLEEN WILLEY

⭐ Kathleen was the widow of a Virginia lawyer and a White House volunteer. In November 1993, she claimed, she went to the president to ask him for a full-time job. A short time into the meeting, according to her, Clinton took her into the hallway between his private pantry and the Oval Office, kissed her, put his hand on her breast, put her hand on his crotch and sighed, "I wanted to do that for a long time." Kathleen left quickly. She was later hired by the White House and sent as a delegate to two international summits. (NOTE: Monica Lewinsky later claimed that president said the charges were ludicrous because he would never approach a small-breasted woman like Kathleen.)

## OTHERS SAY THE DUMBEST THINGS ABOUT BILL CLINTON

# JUDITH KRANTZ

⭐ After popular writer Judith Krantz met President Clinton in 1994, she offered this assessment: "Shaking hands with Bill Clinton is, in and of itself, a full-body sexual experience, I promise you. He has the sexiest handshake of any man that I have ever experienced in my life."

# TYLER PETERSON

⭐ On the 1993 thirtieth anniversary of Bill Clinton's White House meeting with Pres. John F. Kennedy, Clinton hosted a meeting of his own with Boys Nation delegates. One delegate, Tyler Peterson, gave the following assessment of meeting the president: "Meeting him, shaking his hand—it was overwhelming. It was better than sex." The teenager paused. "Of course, I haven't had sex before, but I'm sure this was better."

# Hillary Rodham Clinton

## FACTS OF LIFE

ORIGIN: Born Hillary Diane Rodham, October 26, 1947, Chicago, Illinois.

FORMATIVE YEARS: Wellesley College, B.A., 1969; Yale Law School, J.D., 1973. (Delayed graduation for a year so she could graduate with her boyfriend Bill Clinton.)

FAMILY PLANNING: Married Bill Clinton (lawyer), October 11, 1975. (She changed her name to Hillary Rodham Clinton in 1985.)

SELECTED ELECTION SCORECARD: 2000: potential candidate for U.S. Senate, New York.

## QUICKIE BIO

According to White House legend, President Clinton and First Lady Hillary once pulled into a gas station. As it turned out, the guy who pumped their fuel was one of Hillary's old high-school boyfriends. Bill joked, "If you had married him, you'd be married to a gas-station attendant." Hillary responded, "No, I'd be married to the president of the United States."

Born to a drapery maker and raised in suburban Chicago, Hillary Clinton was a competitive and brilliant student who went to Wellesley College and became head of the local chapter of the Young Republicans. Oops! By the time she entered Yale Law School and met her future husband Bill Clinton in the library, she had become a liberal Democrat.

After graduating from Yale, Hillary went to work for the House Judiciary Committee preparing documents for the impeachment of President Nixon in 1974. She turned down several lucrative offers in order to travel back to Arkansas with her boyfriend Bill Clinton and supervise his unsuccessful 1974 campaign for Congress. The next year she married Clinton, and helped him become governor. After he lost his bid for gubernatorial reelection, Hillary adopted his last name and underwent a beauty makeover, something she would continue to do for the next twenty years. As America's first lady, Hillary set out to be a major policy maker, but instead became "the Hillary problem." When her campaign for national health reform died in 1995, she turned her attention to traveling, writing books, and positioning herself to run for the Senate from New York, a state in which she had never lived. As one of the cooks at the Arkansas governor's mansion noted, "The devil's in that woman."

## HILLARY RODHAM CLINTON DOES THE DUMBEST THINGS

✪ In 1969, Hillary gave the first student commencement address in the history of Wellesley College. "We talk about reality," she babbled, "and I would like to talk about reality sometime, authentic reality, inauthentic reality . . . " She went on to say that she and her classmates were "searching for more immediate, ecstatic and penetrating modes of living."

✪ Hillary searched for a more penetrating mode of living in 1975 when she visited a recruiting office in Fayetteville, Arkansas, and asked about joining the Marine Corps. She claimed she was told to forget it: "You're too old, you can't see, and you're a woman. Maybe the dogs [the Army] would take you." Later that same year, she wed Bill Clinton.

✪ On at least one occasion while she was the first lady of Arkansas, Hillary had members of her security detail fetch sanitary napkins from her bathroom in the governor's mansion and deliver them to her law office.

✪ At times, Hillary liked to greet people with nifty phrases like, "What's up, buttercup?" and "You're as cute as a bug in a rug." But when she caught husband Bill flirting, a trooper supposedly heard her say, "Come on, Bill, put your dick up. You can't f*** her here."

✪ "People are mean," observed Hillary, who expected state troopers to clean up after Socks the cat, who frequently puked on the floor of the governor's mansion.

★ In 1978, Hillary met campaign worker Juanita Broderick at a political rally. Broderick claimed that Clinton had sexually attacked her a few weeks before. But at the fund-raiser, Broderick recalled shaking Hillary's hand. "I'm so happy to meet you," Hillary told her. "I want you to know that we appreciate everything you do for Bill."

★ Since the 1980s, Hillary has received hundreds of thousands of dollars in tax deductions for charitable contributions. Among the things she contributed to charity—the Clintons' used underwear.

★ After Hillary invested in the Whitewater real-estate development in 1981, she wrote, "If Reaganomics works at all, Whitewater could become the Western Hemisphere's Mecca." Not only was Whitewater a terrible investment, but Hillary became the first first lady to be subpoenaed by a federal grand jury for her involvement in the deal. The investigation of Whitewater eventually led to the impeachment and trial of Hillary's husband, President Bill.

★ Hillary brought three lawyers with her from Arkansas to Washington; Bernard Nussbaum, who supposedly had to resign over the Travelgate scandal; Webster Hubbell, who was convicted of tax fraud and sent to prison; and Vince Foster, who committed suicide.

★ Reportedly, it was common knowledge around Little Rock that Hillary and attorney Vince Foster had been very close. State troopers knew that Foster frequently visited Hillary at the governor's mansion when Bill was away. One trooper later recalled a night out with Bill and Hillary and Foster and his wife, as well as a friend, Beth Coulson, and her husband. The lawman alleged that Vince and Hillary were "running tongues down each other's throats, the whole nine yards." The trooper described the scene as "a diagonal swap."

★ One guard claimed he heard Hillary tell Governor Bill, "Bill, I need to be f***ed more than twice a year." One of Clinton's alleged mistresses said that Bill didn't like to have sex with Hillary because, supposedly, Hillary only enjoyed the missionary position.

★ In January 1992, after Gennifer Flowers went public with her accusation that she had had a twelve-year-long affair with Clinton, Bill and Hillary appeared on TV's *60 Minutes,* right after the Super Bowl. "I'm not sitting here because I'm some little woman standing by her man, like Tammy Wynette," Hillary declared. Later she apologized. "I didn't mean to hurt Tammy as a person. I happen to enjoy country music."

In 1996 First Lady Hillary Clinton posed with New York mayor Rudy Giuliani in front of a statue of former first lady Eleanor Roosevelt. Hillary liked to have in-depth discussions with long-dead Eleanor, whom she found to be much more sympathetic than Rudy.
(Courtesy of Reuters/Jeff Christensen/ Archive Photos)

✪ Later, Hillary accused George H. W. Bush of purportedly having an affair with a woman named Jennifer (with a J). "You know, I just don't understand why they think they can get away with this," Hillary fumed. "Everybody knows about George Bush."

✪ After the midterm elections in 1994, Bill and Hillary invited five self-help writers to Camp David to help figure out why the Republicans had won a majority in the House of Representatives. One was Jean Houston, who claimed to have had conversations with the Greek goddess Athena, her "spiritual partner." When Hillary confessed that she had had imaginary discussions with Eleanor Roosevelt, Houston declared that Eleanor was Hillary's "spiritual partner," and guided Hillary through a series of conversations with the long-deceased first lady. Hillary was so impressed with the experience that she invited Houston to move into the White House and help write the book *It Takes a Village: And Other Lessons Children Teach Us* (1996).

✪ In August 1999, Bill Clinton offered clemency to sixteen Puerto Rican nationalists, a move that pleased the 1.3 million Puerto Ricans in New York City, where Hillary was campaigning for U.S. Senate. But when the clemency offer was met with a furious reaction from other New York Democrats, Hillary asked her husband the chief executive to take it back. He didn't. Hillary's opponent, New York City Mayor Rudy Giuliani quipped, "Sometimes it's stand by him, sometimes it's stand against him. It's getting confusing now."

# Christopher Dodd

## FACTS OF LIFE

**ORIGIN:** Born Christopher John Dodd, Willimantic, Connecticut, May 27, 1944.

**FORMATIVE YEARS:** Providence College, B.A., 1966; University of Louisville School of Law, J.D., 1972.

**FAMILY PLANNING:** Married Susan Mooney (worked for his father), 1970; divorced, 1982; married Jackie Marie Clegg (banker), June 18, 1999.

**SELECTED ELECTION SCORECARD:** 1974–78: won, U.S. House of Representatives, 7th District, Connecticut. 1980–98: won, U.S. Senate, Connecticut.

## QUICKIE BIO

I'm not politically driven," explained Chris Dodd in the early 1980s. Yeah, sure. And Bianca Jagger wasn't a hottie. Dodd's father was a liberal Democrat whose career ended after he was censured by the Senate in 1967. Son Chris was in the Peace Corps in the Dominican Republic at the time, but returned and worked on his dad's failed reelection bid in 1970. Dodd became a lawyer, then was asked to run for Congress by an old friend of his parent. Chris won a seat in the U.S. Senate, where a reporter commented that he looked like "the guy in college who recently cut his hair for the first job interview." After his divorce in 1982, Chris and his big buddy Sen. Teddy Kennedy

(D-Massachusetts) earned a reputation as the hardest-partying, skirt-chasing hell-raisers in the Senate. When asked in the 1990s about Chris and Ted's excellent 1980s adventures, an older, wiser Dodd sighed, "God, I hate these questions!" Party on, Chris.

## CHRIS DODD DOES
## THE DUMBEST THINGS

✪ During the 1978 Democratic midterm convention in Memphis, Tennessee, young Congressman Dodd drank with buddies at a hotel bar until closing time, then hopped on a bus and headed for Graceland, Elvis Presley's mansion. Dodd and the gang next headed to a Dunkin' Donuts. Chris told the waitress, "Don't worry," then climbed behind the counter and started handing out donuts to his pals. A food fight erupted, and continued even after Dodd and his fellow Democrats reboarded their bus.

✪ Dodd was quite interested in foreign affairs, as well as supposedly *having affairs* with foreigners. His interest in Central American issues peaked as he was dating Bianca Jagger, the ex-wife of Rolling Stone's Mick Jagger and a native of Nicaragua. Reportedly, Dodd and Bianca discussed political strategy between bouts of lovemaking, while FBI agents reportedly listened via electronic surveillance.

✪ As the Democratic National Committee co-chairman, Dodd delivered a stirring speech in support of the Democrat who was planning to run against Sen. Strom Thurmond (R-South Carolina): "We've got a strong candidate," Dodd declared. "I'm trying to think of his name."

✪ One evening, Ted Kennedy and Dodd were dining at La Colline, a French restaurant in the Washington, D.C., area. Kennedy spotted a picture of Dodd on the wall and shouted, "Who's this guy?" Then Kennedy laughed and threw the picture on the floor. Chris saw Teddy's photo on the wall and did the same thing. Then they proceeded to do a Mexican hat dance on the photos.

✪ On another night out at La Colline, a feeling-no-pain Dodd and an equally numbed Kennedy played Zorro, crossing gladiolas in a mock swordfight.

✪ In 1985, Chris had dinner at the chic Washington restaurant La Brasserie with Teddy Kennedy and two young blondes. The four occupied a private dining room. When the women split for the ladies' room, Teddy called in a waitress, reportedly pulling her onto the table right in the middle of all the food. When the server tried to regain her footing,

Kennedy picked her up and put her on Chris's lap. Then Teddy leaned over the woman and began rubbing against her. Another server entered, saw the senator-waitress-senator sandwich, and screamed for help. When assistance arrived, Dodd looked around and declared, "It's not my fault." Teddy broke into a goofy grin and commented, "Makes you wonder about the leaders of the country."

✪ One night, Teddy was entertaining a companion in the bedroom of his home in McLean, Virginia, when he was startled by a rap at the window. Reportedly, he looked out and saw Dodd carrying a bottle of champagne, accompanied by two nude women. Chris yelled at Teddy that he wanted to use Teddy's Jacuzzi.

✪ After hearing Anita Hill's testimony against Supreme Court nominee Clarence Thomas, in which Hill claimed Thomas spoke to her about porn stars, Dodd told the Senate, "Sexual harassment is an issue that deserves far more attention than has been given over the past number of years in this country."

# Henry B. Gonzalez

**DUMBEST QUOTES**

"Piojos, háganse a un lado, aqui viene su peine."
("Lice, step aside, here comes your comb.")

"Drink their beer and eat their tamales,
but when you go to the polls, vote for Gonzalez."

## FACTS OF LIFE

**ORiGiN:** Born Henry Barbosa Gonzalez, May 3, 1916, San Antonio, Texas.

**FORMATIVE YEARS:** Attended University of Texas; St. Mary's University School of Law, B.A. and LL.B., 1943.

**FAMiLY PLANNiNG:** Married Bertha Cuellar, November 1940.

**SELECTED ELECTiON SCORECARD:** 1958: lost, governor, Texas. 1961: lost, U.S. Senate, Texas. 1961–96: won, U.S. House of Representatives, 20th District, Texas.

## QUICKIE BIO

As they used to sing in San Antonio, *"Don't mess with Henry / Don't call him no Commie / He'll send you home / Crying to Mommy . . ."* Like Davy Crockett, Daniel Boone, and the other battlers who went down fighting at San Antonio's Alamo in 1836, Henry B. marched to his own mariachi beat. Gonzalez's father was the former mayor of a town in Mexico who escaped a firing squad and then fled his native country during the 1911 revolution. The elder Gonzalez settled in San Antonio and edited what was, for many years, the only Spanish-language newspaper in the U.S. Henry worked as a probation officer and a translator in San Antonio before becoming the first Hispanic in more than a century to serve in the Texas state senate and the first Mexican-American to go to Congress from Texas. Henry B. fought for civil rights in Texas and the nation, but by the time he retired from politics at age eighty-two, he seemed more interested in pontificating than passing legislation. "He is more like a leek than an onion," a workmate observed of Henry B. "There are a lot of layers but also some interesting offshoots."

## HENRY B. GONZALEZ DOES
## THE DUMBEST THINGS

★ Henry B. was a boxer in college, and liked to throw punches. In 1963, when Rep. Ed Foreman (R-Texas) called him a "pinko," Gonzalez chased after him, confronted him in the cloakroom, and pushed him. "I'm not going to let a little two-bit, loudmouthed, mad-dog type of guy talk to me that way," Henry B. explained, "even if he is from Texas."

★ In 1986, another man called Henry B. a communist at a restaurant in San Antonio. The seventy-year-old congressman gave him a black eye, despite the fact that the guy was forty-six and carried a nine-inch deer-gutting knife. Gonzalez claimed the attack was part of a Republican conspiracy, and observed, "Who was going to help me once I was gutted?"

★ Gonzalez was a conspiracy theorist who saw a definite link between the assassinations of Pres. John Kennedy and African-American civil-rights leader Martin Luther King Jr. In 1977 he headed a special House panel to investigate their deaths. Henry B. wound up accusing the panel's chief counsel of being "an unscrupulous individual, an unconscionable scoundrel." He then fired the chief counsel and claimed that organized crime was ruining the investigation, and resigned from the panel.

★ In the 1980s, Gonzalez was chairman of the House Banking Subcommittee on Housing. He combated the Reagan administration over cutting back on housing, and fought especially hard with Samuel Riley Pierce Jr., Reagan's Secretary of Housing and Urban Development. At one point Henry B. called the black cabinet member "Stepin Fetchit."

★ On his desk at Congress, Henry B. displayed a placard with the words, "Se Habla Ingles" (English spoken here).

★ Gonzalez introduced articles of impeachment against Pres. Ronald Reagan—twice.

⭐ Henry B. introduced articles of impeachment against George H. W. Bush—once. Gonzalez accused President Bush of wooing Iraqi leader Saddam Hussein with agricultural loans and hi-tech goods before the 1991 Gulf War erupted. The congressman spent three years investigating his accusations under the authority of the House Banking and Financial Services Committee. Republicans accused Henry of holding a "kangaroo court." Gonzalez selectively released classified documents to support his claims until the U.S. attorney general cut off his access to such data.

⭐ Gonzalez was a civil-rights leader in the 1950s. However, by the 1960s his methods were criticized by the more radical Chicano leaders. In 1962, when Henry B. heard that another Chicano politician had said he was a traitor to his people, Gonzalez told him, "You either cut that out or I'll knock the s*** out of you." Gonzalez later apologized.

⭐ In 1973, Gonzalez got into even more trouble while attempting to give a lecture at a college in Boulder, Colorado. Henry B. claimed that before his speech, he was hustled into a room by a group of young people who said that he was "on trial" and demanded that he denounce "the gringo establishment and the mistreatment of Chicanos." Finally, Gonzalez had enough and yelled, "One thing I never take from anybody is s***. To hell with you. Screw you. You think you're gonna scare me!" When a youth approached doubling a fist, Gonzalez told him, "You get your big a** over there and don't stand on my right, or else I might have to knock the s*** out of you."

⭐ That evening, the protestors appeared at Gonzalez's lecture. One jumped onto the stage and threw the mike away. Henry B. believed that several of the instigators were carrying pistols. He looked at one of the armed protestors and said, "Hey, son, I've got you picked out. You may kill me, but I've got you picked out to go with me, because I'll kill you first." Gonzalez and his host decided not to call in the police because it might have made things worse. So the politician asked his host's wife to pretend to faint. When she did, Gonzalez and his host helped her out of the room, and escaped the mob.

⭐ In his last years in office, Gonzalez loved to talk late at night to an empty chamber. His motto? "Keep making speeches and eventually people will hear you."

# Al Gore

## FACTS OF LIFE

ORIGIN: Born Albert Gore Jr., March 31, 1948, Washington, D.C.

FORMATIVE YEARS: Harvard University, B.A., 1969; Vanderbilt University Graduate School of Religion, 1971–72, never graduated; Vanderbilt University Law School, 1974–76, never graduated.

FAMILY PLANNING: Married Mary Elizabeth "Tipper" Aitcheson (high school sweetheart/photographer), May 19, 1970.

SELECTED ELECTION SCORECARD: 1976–82: won, U.S. House of Representatives, 4th District, Tennessee. 1984: won, U.S. Senate, Tennessee. 1984–88: lost, U.S. president. 1992–96: won, U.S. vice president under Pres. Bill Clinton. 1996–2000: won, U.S. vice president under Pres. Bill Clinton. 2000: potential candidate for U.S. president.

## QUICKIE BIO

The worst sin in politics," Richard Nixon once declared, "is being boring." Oh, Al, you sinner! But it's not all his fault. Al Gore was born and raised to be a sensible policy wonk. The son of Sen. Al Gore Sr. from Tennessee, Al Jr. was born in Washington, D.C., and went to Harvard. He tried to act wild, but never quite pulled it off. He marched against the Vietnam War, but joined the Army. He served in Vietnam, but as a reporter, not a soldier. He did graduate work in religion at Vanderbilt, but switched to law; then dropped that and entered politics. Handsome, articulate, hardworking, serious, a dedicated husband, and a self-described "raging moderate," Gore repeatedly ran for president, but was just not dumb enough to win. Even President Clinton admitted that his vice president was dull. After he named Gore to head an important government initiative, the chief executive explained. "I asked him to do it because he was the only person I could trust to read all 150,000 pages in the Code of Federal Regulations."

Go, Al, go!

## AL GORE DOES
## THE DUMBEST THINGS

★ In the fall of 1985 Tipper Gore, who once played drums for an all-girl band called the Wildcats, spearheaded a drive to ban nasty rock lyrics and helped convince the Senate Commerce Committee to hold hearings on the subject. During the hearings, Sen. Al Gore told Frank Zappa, who once wrote a song about eating "yellow snow," "I have been a fan of your music, believe it or not, and I respect you as a true original and tremendously talented musician." Al told John Denver, who wrote a song about taking LSD in the Rocky Mountains, "I have been a fan for a long time, Mr. Denver." Then Dee Snider of the band Twisted Sister, who was also present, asked Senator Al, "Excuse me, are you gonna tell me you're a big fan of my music as well?" Gore admitted he was "not a fan" of Twisted Sister.

★ At a Hollywood party in the 1990s, Gore found himself talking to Courtney Love, the lead singer of the band Hole. Gore tried to charm the rocker by saying that he was a really big fan of her music. "Yeah right," Love responded, "name a song, Al." "I can't name a song," Gore burbled, "I'm just a really big fan."

★ In 1987, Tipper and Al admitted that they had smoked grass, but said they regretted it. In 1999, Tipper played drums with the legendary rock band the Grateful Dead. The Dead didn't regret it.

★ After the Chicago Bulls won its sixth NBA championship in 1998, rocking Vice President Gore gushed, "I tell you, that Michael Jackson is unbelievable, isn't he? He's just unbelievable."

★ Gore told reporters from *Time* magazine in 1997 that the popular Erich Segal novel *Love Story* was actually based on the romance between Al and Tipper. Segal denied it, but did say that the male character in the story was partially based on Al. "He was always under pressure to follow in his father's footsteps. . . ."

★ In the spring of 1988, Gore the environmentalist phoned the *Washington Post* with an important announcement. "I just had to call," the senator said, "because you've printed a picture of the Earth upside down on the front page of the paper." Sorry, Al. There is no up or down in space.

"I didn't realize I was in a Buddhist temple," Al Gore claimed in 1996 after attending a political fundraiser where contributions were illegally solicited. It sure looked like a Buddhist temple to everyone else.

(Courtesy of Reuters/Rick Wilking/Archive Photos)

⭐ Al wrote a best-selling book about the environment entitled *Earth in the Balance: Ecology and the Human Spirit* (1993). He later proposed to spend $32 million to have a live video image of the Earth available twenty-four hours a day on the Internet. Republicans were quick to distribute a list of Internet sites that already carried images of the Earth from space.

⭐ When a woman from Texas wrote to Vice President Gore, complaining about the fact that the Texas Eagle train service had been terminated, environmentalist Gore wrote back: "I share your view that the urgent problem of species extinction and the conservation of biological diversity should be addressed. All plants and animals help make our natural surroundings more diverse and should be protected."

⭐ In March 1996, Vice President Al Gore gave a speech in Denver and stood for photos in front of the South Platte River. The river was low, so the city released ninety-six million gallons of water into the river for the photo op. The water was worth about $59,000.

⭐ Three years later, officials released water into the drought-stricken Connecticut River to ensure that Gore's canoe would remain afloat during a photo opportunity to promote environmental awareness.

⭐ At the 1996 Democratic Convention in Chicago, Gore sought to change his lackluster public image by speaking of the personal crises that had changed his life. One incident concerned his sister, who died of lung cancer in 1984. He said her passing spurred him to fight the tobacco industry. Huh? Gore himself was a tobacco farmer. While campaigning for president in 1988, he claimed, "Throughout most of my life, I raised tobacco. I want you to know that with my own hands, all of my life, I put it in the plant beds and transferred it. I've hoed it. I've chopped it. I've shredded it, spiked it, put it in the barn and stripped it and sold it." Gore even accepted campaign contributions from the tobacco industry until 1990, six years after his sister's death.

✪ In an Oval Office meeting prior to President Clinton's first Thanksgiving Day turkey pardoning, Clinton worried that the turkey might pee on him. In response, Gore offered to demonstrate his ability to hypnotize the big birds.

✪ While listening to an Al Gore speech, domestic-science maven Martha Stewart closed her eyes. Later she explained, "I'm going through eye-exercise therapy, strengthening my eyes. I'm supposed to . . . rest them."

✪ Gore read the French philosopher Maurice Merleau-Ponty's book *Phenomenology of Perception* (1992) and explained that it helped him "in cultivating a capacity for a more refined introspection that gave me better questions that ultimately led to a renewed determination to become involved with the effort to make things better."

✪ In March 1999, Gore declared, "During my service in the United States Congress, I took the initiative in creating the Internet." Sorry, Al! The Internet was created in the 1960s, before Gore entered politics. Later Al admitted to a steelworker in Pittsburgh that he had "trouble turning on a computer, let along using one."

✪ When Gore's campaign unveiled its Web site to the press in 1999, it showed off a "Just for Kids" section that asked for children's names, e-mail addresses, and zip codes. A reporter pointed out that Congress had outlawed collecting such data in 1998 to protect children from child molesters.

✪ Feminist writer Naomi Wolf denied that she was encouraging presidential candidate Al Gore to be a dominant "Alpha male" instead of a subordinate "Beta male." But she did not deny that Al Gore paid her $15,000 a week for ten months in 1999 so that he could listen to the "women's voices" that she claimed to "carry around" with her. At times, Wolf hopped around in a circle to emphasize how important it was that Gore be elected president.

# Gary Hart

## FACTS OF LIFE

ORIGIN: Born Gary Warren Hartpence, November 28, 1937, Ottawa, Kansas. (He later changed his last name to Hart.)

FORMATIVE YEARS: Bethany Nazarene College, B.A., 1958; Yale Divinity School, B.D., 1961; Yale School of Law, LL.B., 1964.

FAMILY PLANNING: Married Lee Ludwig, 1958.

SELECTED ELECTION SCORECARD: 1974–80: won, U.S. Senate, Colorado. 1984–88: lost, U.S. president.

## QUICKIE BIO

Gary Hart started out to become a minister and got sidetracked—way sidetracked. Born to a farming family, Gary attended divinity school and then law school. He worked in Washington, D.C., before returning to Colorado in 1967 to teach environmental law, and then to start his own law practice. Hart was the mastermind behind the 1972 presidential campaign of Sen. George S. McGovern (D-South Dakota), one of the biggest disasters in Democratic presidential history. Gary went on to even greater disasters on his own. He ran unsuccessfully for president in 1984, and owed $1.3 million in campaign debt when he announced that he was going to run again for the office in 1987. "If I am elected I won't be the first adulterer in the White House,"

Hart proclaimed in January 1988, after admitting that he had an affair. "I may be the first one to have publicly confessed." Sorry, Gary. That honor eventually went to Pres. Bill Clinton.

## GARY HART DOES THE DUMBEST THINGS

✪ Hart was named Hartpence. But when he entered politics he changed his name to Hart. Why? In part to avoid being called by his childhood nickname, "Hot Pants." Gary also altered his birthdate on his résumé, from 1937 to 1936.

✪ When he announced his candidacy for the presidency in 1983, Gary Hart asserted he represented a "new political generation" with "new ideas." His advisors had to remind him to kiss his wife Lee, from whom he had been separated—twice.

✪ Hart's basic campaign speech mentioned "new strategies," "new ways," "new help," "new job skills," "new path," and a "new generation of leadership." One of Gary's supporters observed, "He does have new ideas, even though I can't remember exactly what they are." Said another, "Hart. John Hart. I like him." The press dubbed Hart "his newness."

✪ At a public appearance with his wife in 1984, Gary said, "She campaigns in California and I campaign in New Jersey." His wife quipped, "I got to hold a koala bear." Hart added, "I won't tell you what I got to hold. Samples of a toxic-waste dump." Three days later, he apologized to the people of New Jersey.

✪ At the Democratic convention (held in San Francisco) in July 1984, Hart proclaimed, "This is one Hart you won't leave in San Francisco." The Democrats nominated Sen. Walter Mondale (D-Minnesota) for the presidential ticket.

✪ When Gary announced his intention to seek the Democratic nomination for the presidency in 1987, he warned his supporters, "As a candidate, I can almost guarantee that I'm going to make some mistakes."

✪ Hart challenged the media in May 1987: "If anybody wants to put a tail on me, go ahead. They'd be very bored." Journalists from the *Miami Herald* accepted the challenge, followed him to his Washington townhouse, and reported that he had spent the night there with a woman who was *not* his spouse.

✪ Hart told reporters staked outside his home that he and the woman in question had "no personal relationship."

- Hart later identified the female as Donna Rice, and claimed that he did nothing "immoral." When asked about a trip to Bimini Island in the Bahamas with Ms. Rice aboard the chartered yacht *Monkey Business*, Gary explained that the men and women slept on separate boats. When questioned about a photo that showed Donna sitting on his lap and laughing, the politician explained later, "The attractive lady whom I had only recently been introduced to dropped into my lap. I chose not to dump her off."

- When asked if he had ever committed adultery, Hart responded, "I do not have to answer that question."

- After cavorting aboard the vessel *Monkey Business*, Donna Rice refused to tell TV interviewer Barbara Walters whether she had been intimate with the former presidential candidate, saying, "It's a question of dignity." Donna later got a gig as a TV spokesperson for No Excuses jeans. Her pitch line, "I make no excuses—I only wear them."

- Hart dropped out of the presidential race in May 1987, then dropped back into the contest in December 1987. Why? To collect the federal matching funds he needed to retire his campaign debt. He vacated the race permanently in May 1988 and returned home—to Troublesome Gulch, Colorado.

- Gary said that his victimization by the media changed his life. "Black people come up to me on the street," he claimed, "and want to shake my hand."

- After his 1988 presidential run, Gary Hart held up a copy of the Disney animated classic *Dumbo* (1941) in a video store and declared, "This is a documentary of my campaign."

# Rev. Jesse Jackson

## FACTS OF LIFE

**ORIGIN:** Born Jesse Burns (later adopted by stepfather Charles Jackson), October 8, 1941, Greenville, South Carolina.

**FORMATIVE YEARS:** North Carolina Agricultural and Technical College, B.A., 1964; Chicago Theological Seminary, dropped out.

**FAMILY PLANNING:** Married Jacqueline Lavinia Brown (college student), January 31, 1962.

**SELECTED ELECTION SCORECARD:** 1984–88: lost, U.S. president.

## QUICKIE BIO

Just what are we supposed to do with this guy?" asked a frustrated U.S. Embassy official when Jesse Jackson descended on him overseas. Nobody could really figure out what to do with Jesse. Born out-of-wedlock to a sixteen-year-old woman and her thirty-something neighbor, Jesse Jackson was an outstanding athlete who quit the University of Illinois football team, and worked alongside civil-rights leader Martin Luther King Jr. Later Jesse became a preacher without a church, and a grassroots organizer who once hosted TV's *Saturday Night Live*. In 1983, Rev. Jackson traveled to Syria and secured the release of a black American pilot. After that, Jesse transformed himself into an unofficial U.S. diplomat. He hugged Yasser Arafat, interviewed Saddam Hussein, and negotiated for the release of American soldiers in Serbia. He was a world-renowned politician who never won an election. Above all else, Jesse Jackson was, and is, a talker. According to one friend, Jackson "could talk a hole through a billy goat." Organizations like Operation Breadbasket, People United to Save Humanity (PUSH), and the National Rainbow Coalition supported Jackson. But where exactly did the money come from? According to Jesse, "The Rainbow! The Rainbow!"

## REV. JESSE JACKSON DOES THE DUMBEST THINGS

✪ At twenty-four, Jackson became the youngest aide of Martin Luther King Jr. and spent a year and a half working with the great civil-rights leader. Jesse was at the Lorraine Motel in Memphis, Tennessee, when King was assassinated there. Later Jesse told a TV crew that he had cradled Dr. King's head in his arms as the civil-rights leader passed away. Others who were at the scene suggest that Jackson created the whole narrative. One eyewitness suggested that Jackson hid behind the motel swimming pool when the shooting began, and flew to Chicago a few hours later, saying, "I'm sick. . . ."

✪ Jackson may not have held the dying King's head, but he did manage to get Martin Luther King Jr.'s blood on his shirt. Jesse wore the bloody shirt for an appearance on the TV program *Today*.

✪ Jesse sees himself as a part of history. At different times he has compared himself to Martin Luther King Jr. and Rudolph the Red-nosed Reindeer. "Rudolph had to do more than the other reindeer to get his recognition," Jesse declared. "Rudolph's pullin' the most weight. But Santa says, 'Well, we thank you Rudolph. 'Course, no promotion, no equity, no vice presidential nomination . . .' "

✪ In the mid-1980s, when Jackson's staff hadn't been paid in three weeks, Jesse still chose to fly back from Europe with four of his children and several assistants on the Concorde, at a cost of $2,000 per seat. When

Jesse Jackson liked to say that a black president "couldn't mess the world up no worse than these sick white cats."
(Courtesy of Darlene Hammond/Pictorial Parade/ Archive Photos)

asked why he didn't opt for a cheaper flight, an angry Jesse charged, "You're trying to sabotage my spirit!"

⭐ After meeting with French Pres. François Mitterrand, Jackson told a reporter, "President Mitterrand here says I'm a mystery to him." He then turned to Mitterrand and said, "Go ahead, Mr. President, tell him what you were telling me about bein' a mystery to you."

⭐ Jackson met with communist leader Fidel Castro in Cuba in 1984 and conversed for eight hours. After agreeing to release forty-nine prisoners to the African-American negotiator, Fidel handed Jesse a cigar. Jackson stuck the cigar in his mouth, wrong end first. Fidel plucked the stogie from his visitor's lips, lit it for him, and gave it back.

⭐ Jesse talked so much that even his authorized biographer couldn't stand it. On an airplane flight with Jackson, the writer lay down and pretended to sleep, just to get away from Jesse's political musings.

⭐ A woman who was traveling with Jackson said to one of his supporters, "Jesse's told me we're getting married as soon as he can get free, but he hasn't told me when yet. Has he told you?" Supposedly, the supporter finally left Jackson's service because of "all the adulteries."

- Jackie, Jesse's wife, once accompanied him to South Africa for a meeting with that country's Pres. Frederik de Klerk. "He [Jesse Jackson] suddenly grabbed my arm, pushed me up against the wall—my head banged against the wall—and he said, 'You keep your mouth shut in here.' " They went into the office and President de Klerk asked Jackie if she wanted tea or coffee. Jackie said, "Well, my husband told me I wasn't supposed to open my mouth in here, so I don't guess I can tell you, Mr. President. . . ."

- "I've covered his a** right down the line on that thing," Jackie said about Jesse's claimed extramarital romances. "But do you think he's grateful?" In 1987 she declared, "I would suggest that he take care. That he take care with what he does in the streets so he won't excite the horses."

- When Jesse Jackson was rumored to be considering a run for mayor of Washington, D.C., in 1992, the incumbent Marion Barry said of his potential rival, "Jesse don't wanna run anything but his mouth."

# John Jenrette

## FACTS OF LIFE

**ORIGIN:** Born John Wilson Jenrette Jr., May 19, 1936, Conway, South Carolina.

**FORMATIVE YEARS:** Methodist Men's College, A.B., 1958; University of South Carolina Law School, LL.B., 1962.

**FAMILY PLANNING:** Married first wife and divorced; married Rita Carpenter (researcher), September 10, 1976; divorced, 1981.

**SELECTED ELECTION SCORECARD:** 1972: lost, U.S. House of Representatives, 6th District, South Carolina. 1974–78: won, U.S. House of Representatives, 6th District, South Carolina.

## QUICKIE BIO

Women gain status according to how powerful a man they're sleeping with"—at least, according to Rita Jenrette, who lost all status in Washington, D.C., after she blabbed about her husband John Jenrette. He was a hard-drinking playboy who worked as a lawyer and a judge in the party town of North Myrtle Beach, South Carolina, before winning a seat in Congress in the anti-Republican post-Watergate backlash of the mid-1970s. Jenrette proved to be much more controversial than Watergate. While in Congress, he was investigated for alleged drug smuggling, jury tampering, and selling of underwater real estate, but he was never convicted of any of these allegations. The most outrageous thing about Jenrette was his gorgeous second wife, Rita, who worked as a Republican analyst before marrying the liberal Democrat Jenrette. The good times ended in 1980 with the so-called Abscam scandal, and the revelations by Rita of senatorial "nooners" and quickies in the bowels of the Capitol Building. Of life in the political world with John, Rita bragged once, "I'm proud of having survived."

## JOHN JENRETTE DOES
## THE DUMBEST THINGS

✪ John Jenrette proposed to Rita Carpenter at the 1976 Democratic Convention, held in New York City. Then they went party-hopping. After attending a bash thrown by *Rolling Stone* magazine, the newly engaged Rita found Jenrette on the roof of a building "making out with a woman who must have weighed two hundred pounds." Jenrette explained that he was drunk at the time, and that the female in question was Shirley MacLaine. According to Rita, "She wasn't."

✪ Rita and John once had sexual relations while standing on the steps of the Capitol Building in Washington, D.C. According to her, "John unbuttoned my fur coat, and I fumbled with his zipper. . . . We wrapped my coat around us, and we made love standing in the shadow of the large columns. I remember thinking how cold, very cold, it was, but how warm it was next to John."

✪ While they were supposedly making love in front of the government building, House Speaker Tip O'Neill (D-Massachusetts) passed by and said, "Hi, John. How are you?" The Jenrettes both said fine.

✪ Rita and John visited New Guinea on a congressional junket. He spotted an aboriginal village, jumped out of his car, and walked into it with Rita in tow. The Jenrettes traded some of their clothes for several native objects, including a fertility statue.

✪ Reportedly, in 1979 Jenrette checked into a substance-abuse facility in Texas—for the fourth time. The clinic stressed aversion therapy. John told Rita that this time the treatment was going to work, and he informed the clinicians that he drank scotch. He developed an aversion to scotch, but not to brandy, which he really preferred.

✪ In the late 1970s, the FBI launched Abscam, a sting operation to root out corruption in Washington, D.C. The agency set up an ex-convict disguised as a wealthy sheik in a D.C. house and tried to bribe congressmen. Apparently it wasn't that hard to do. The Arab impostor purportedly offered to pay Jenrette $50,000 if he would help pass a law that would allow him to stay in the U.S. Jenrette fell for the lure like a

South Carolina bass. John was videotaped accepting the money and telling an undercover FBI agent, "I've got larceny in my heart."

★ Rita later found $25,000 in a white athletic sock stuffed into one of John's shoes. She also discovered $1,700 in one of his suits. The politician claimed tearfully that his mother left him part of the money and the rest was Christmas gifts. Rita was inspired by the incident to write and record a country song, "It Gives Me the Low Down Blues Ever Since You Found Money Stashed in My Shoe."

★ In the summer of 1980, Jenrette hatched a scheme to save his political hide. He called former Ugandan "president for life" Idi Amin, who was close to Iranian holy man the Ayatollah Khomeini, and tried to arrange for the release of American hostages in Tehran. Amin said he could do the deal if Jenrette could arrange for Amin's offspring to go to American schools. Jenrette said no problem, then asked Amin how many children he had. Amin said thirty-eight. The deal never happened.

★ After becoming a scandal celebrity, Rita posed in *Playboy* magazine, appeared in TV ads, acted in a number of movies including *Zombie Island Massacre* (1984) in which she had three nude scenes, campaigned for Clairol's Clairesse hair color, joined Norman Vincent Peale's church, wrote books, acted in the play *A Girl's Guide to Chaos*, and worked for a Wall Street brokerage firm. At one point she considered running for Congress from her home state of Texas.

# Lyndon Baines Johnson

## All-American Presidential Bonus Chapter

---

**DUMBEST QUOTES**

"I had more women by accident than [John F.] Kennedy had on purpose."

"Making a speech on economics is lot like pissin' down your leg. It seems hot to you, but it never does to anyone else."

"Being president is like being a jackass in a hail storm. There's nothing to do but stand there and take it."

---

### FACTS OF LIFE (and Death)

ORIGIN: Born August 27, 1908, near Stonewall, Texas; died of heart failure January 22, 1973, San Antonio, Texas.

FORMATIVE YEARS: Southwest Texas State College, B.S., 1930.

FAMILY PLANNING: Married Claudia Alta "Lady Bird" Taylor (journalism student), November 17, 1934.

SELECTED ELECTION SCORECARD: 1937–48: won, U.S. House of Representatives, 10th District, Texas. 1941: lost, U.S. Senate, Texas. 1948–54: won,

U.S. Senate. 1960: won, U.S. vice president under Pres. John F. Kennedy. (Appointed president November 22, 1963, an hour and a half after the assassination of President Kennedy.) 1964: won, U.S. president.

## QUICKIE BIO

Described by his press secretary as "unbelievably gross," Lyndon Baines Johnson was the acknowledged master of pressing the political flesh. With his hugs, back slaps, kisses, grimaces, and evacuations, LBJ redefined the American body politic. Born to a political family in rural central Texas, Johnson worked as a shoeshine boy, an animal trapper, a hired hand, and a schoolteacher before getting a job with the National Youth Administration, one of the many federal programs started by Pres. Franklin Delano Roosevelt. Lyndon wound up marrying a rich girl, winning a seat in the U.S. House of Representatives, and serving in the U.S. Navy. After becoming a U.S. senator, Johnson became the consummate wheeler-dealer. "If LBJ gave you a match for a cigarette," noted a fellow senator, "he wanted a ranch in return." Lyndon resented the Eastern establishment, particularly Bobby Kennedy, whom Johnson described as "mean, bitter, vicious, and an animal in many ways." Lyndon's own animal instincts eventually got him to the presidency, where he made history with the words, "We have the opportunity to move not only toward the rich society and the powerful society, but upward toward the Great Society. . . ." Johnson was on the way to building his Great Society until the Vietnam War brought down his presidency. Bummed by the escalation of the war, and abandoned by his girlfriend of thirty years, Johnson refused to run for reelection as president in 1968, and retired to his ranch in Texas, where he let his hair grow long and hung out with his dogs. "The trouble with Lyndon is that he is a son of a bitch," one of his friends declared. "The next-worse trouble is that he's a great son of a bitch."

## LYNDON BAINES JOHNSON DOES THE DUMBEST THINGS

✪ While in college, Johnson got out of the shower, wrapped his hand around his member, and proclaimed, "Well, I've gotta give Ol' Jumbo some exercise. I wonder who I'll f*** tonight."

✪ In 1948, Lyndon campaigned in the Texas Democratic primary for the U.S. Senate (the winner of which was ensured of taking the election, since the Republican party was not a force in Texas politics then). When the ballots were tallied, one box filled with completed voting forms was missing—that is, Box 13 from the town of Alice in Jim Wells County. Surprise! The votes from Box 13 were all for Lyndon. In fact, the polling list showed 202 voters' names, all written in the same hand with the same pen. Two weeks later, the list disappeared. Out of 900,000 votes cast, Johnson won by eighty-seven of them, earning him the office of U.S. senator and the nickname "Landslide Lyndon."

★ Johnson himself liked to tell the following joke about the Box 13 election: A man saw a Mexican-American boy crying in the street and asked, "What's the matter?" The youth wailed, "My dad did not come to see me." The man declared, "Why son your daddy's been dead these last six years." "I know," the boy sobbed, "but he came back last Tuesday to vote for Lyndon Johnson and he didn't even stop to see me."

★ After hearing a speech by Vice President Richard Nixon, Senator Johnson said, "Boys, I may not know much, but I know the difference between chicken s*** and chicken salad."

★ When George H. W. Bush asked Johnson if he should run for the Senate, Johnson advised, "The difference between being a member of the Senate and a member of the House is the difference between chicken salad and chicken s***."

★ Vice President Johnson called Pres. John F. Kennedy's aides "the Georgetown jelly beans," and claimed that they "didn't have sense enough to pour piss out of a boot with the instructions written on the heel."

★ LBJ loved his initials. After all, they were also his wife's initials, his two daughters' initials, and the initials of his dog Little Beagle Johnson.

★ At one point, Lyndon posed for pictures, holding up one of his beagles by the ears. When the public reacted with fury, Johnson was baffled, "All I was doing was holding the beagle up so they could get the front of his picture instead of his a**. . . ." He further fumed, "I stand my damn dogs up and hold them by the ears so an AP photographer can get a picture and another little guy that didn't know what he was doing, he writes a story that it is cruel to the dogs. Hell, I know more about hounds than he ever heard of! But they've got every dog lover in the country raising hell, thinking I'm burning them at the stake."

★ After having his gall bladder and a kidney stone removed, the president couldn't resist the urge to pull up his shirt and display his stomach for magazine photographers. "What we had here," said the Leader of the Free World, pointing to his fresh scar, "was two operations for the price of one. . . . There are footprints everywhere that hand went, and I can still feel them."

✪ Johnson didn't want to talk about Vietnam in public and explained, "If you have a mother-in-law with only one eye and she has it in the center of her forehead, you don't keep her in the living room."

✪ Just a few days after dealing with the Gulf of Tonkin Resolution, one of the most critical foreign-affairs emergencies of the Vietnam War, President Johnson was at his ranch in Texas, more worried about his pants than foreign policy. On the phone to Joseph Haggar, chairman of the Haggar Company in Dallas, Johnson ordered six pairs of slacks for summer wear. "The crotch, down there where your nuts hang, is always a little too tight," Lyndon complained to the clothing industrialist. "Give me an inch that I can let out there because they cut me. They're just like riding a wire fence."

✪ As vice president in the early 1960s, Lyndon complained that he was no better than a "cut dog," that is, a dog whose balls had been whacked off.

✪ When Vice President Johnson toured Asia, he invited a Pakistani camel driver to visit the White House, shouted to get an echo in the Taj Mahal, and walked through a slum in India handing out campaign pencils. At a restroom in Thailand, Lyndon whipped it out and asked rhetorically, "Don't see 'em this big out here, do they?"

✪ Johnson had an audience with the Pope and presented the Holy Father with a plastic bust of himself.

✪ Driving around his ranch, Johnson stopped and took a piss in the underbrush. One of the TV reporters asked, "Aren't you afraid a rattlesnake might bite it?" "Hell," Lyndon snorted, "it is part rattlesnake."

✪ Those who were close to the president often wished they didn't have to be. He had the habit of inviting colleagues into the lavatory for a combination bowel movement and strategy session. Sometimes Johnson enjoyed receiving staff briefings and enemas at the same time.

✪ Sen. Hubert Humphrey (D-Minnesota) once pulled up his pants to display the cuts on his shins where Johnson had kicked him yelling, "Get going now!"

✪ Johnson complained about his vice president, Hubert Humphrey, "He cries too much." Lyndon also declared, "He has Minnesota running-water disease. I've never known anyone from Minnesota that could keep their mouth shut. It's just something in the water out there."

✪ "I like for women to like him, and I like him to like them," Lady Bird said about her husband Lyndon. "You have to understand, my husband loved

"I never trust a man unless I got his pecker in my pocket," boasted Lyndon Johnson, shown here with his trusted friend, House Speaker Sam Rayburn (D-Texas).
(Courtesy of the University of Texas, Center for American History)

people. All people. And half the people in the world are women. You don't think I could have kept my husband away from half the people?"

⭐ One Secret Service agent claimed that Lady Bird walked in on the president while he was having sexual relations with someone on a couch in the Oval Office. According to the employee, Johnson had a special alarm installed so that agents could warn him when Lady Bird was coming down the hall. Lyndon was rumored to have had sex with a reporter in the Oval Office as well. One unnamed secretary claimed that she had sex with Johnson atop a desk in the Oval Office.

⭐ Johnson let Ol' Jumbo dip into the company ink. Johnson's aides referred to the secretary pool as his "harem." His press secretary said, "He had the instincts of a Turkish sultan in Istanbul." The major criteria he had for a secretary was beauty. Johnson declared, "I can't stand an ugly woman around or a fat one who looks like a cow that's gonna set on her own udder."

⭐ According to crew members on *Air Force One*, President Johnson had sex with secretaries while locked in the stateroom on the plane even when Lady Bird was on board.

★ Lyndon's favorite pickup line was, "You remind me of my mother!"

★ In 1937, Lyndon met a tall, good-looking woman named Alice Glass, who was the common-law wife of newspaper publisher Charles E. Marsh. Johnson had an affair with her that lasted almost thirty years. At one time, Marsh was drunk and accused Lyndon of "shacking up" with his wife, then later acted as if nothing happened. Alice got furious at Lyndon's escalation of the Vietnam War and dumped him in 1967.

★ Advertising executive Madeleine Brown claimed that she had a twenty-one-year-long affair with Johnson. Madeleine insisted that their relationship was "purely physical." When they first met, she said Lyndon "looked at me like I was an ice cream cone on a hot day." They allegedly had sex the same afternoon. She described his sex style as "rough," "a little kinky," and "commanding."

★ Madeleine got angry when she learned she wasn't Johnson's only girlfriend. Lyndon soothed her by saying, "Today's today, tomorrow's tomorrow." When she got pregnant in 1950, Johnson supposedly yelled, "How could you be such a Dumb Dora?"

★ Madeleine Brown claimed that Lyndon bought her a home with a live-in maid, unlimited credit cards, and a new car every two years.

★ Johnson gave Rep. Adam Clayton Powell Jr. (D-New York) a cigarette lighter. The president said, "Now, Adam, don't go losing this in no whorehouse." Powell answered, "Mr. President, Adam Clayton Powell doesn't have to buy p***y."

★ President Johnson signed the Civil Rights Act in 1964. But the architect of the Great Society didn't always sound so great. Lyndon complained about the budget for Washington, D.C., and "puttin in all this money for these illegitimate women." "They want to just stay up there and breed and won't work and we have to feed them," Johnson declared. "I don't want to be taking any taxpayers' money and paying it to people just to breed."

★ LBJ asked former John F. Kennedy staffer Sargent Shriver, who was director of the Peace Corps at the time, to lead the war on poverty. When he called Shriver to say that he was going to tell the press of his appointment, Sargent asked for a few days to think things over. Lyndon refused to give him the requested time and challenged him by saying, "You've got the power, you've got the money. Now you may not have the glands." Shriver defended himself by saying, "I've got plenty of glands." "I'd like to have your glands, then," the president said, "I need Dr.

Brinkley myself—get some of those goat glands." (Dr. Brinkley was a doctor in Del Rio, Texas, who made a fortune curing male impotency by transplanting goat glands into the male scrotum.)

★ Lyndon liked to discuss the sex lives of bulls while drinking beer and cruising through his Texas ranch in a Lincoln Continental. To stir things up, Johnson would park next to a group of cattle, and push a button that connected to a horn under the hood which made a cowlike mooing sound.

★ Johnson often took reporters with him while he cruised about his ranch spread. When a journalist complained about the ninety-mile-per-hour speed, Lyndon removed his cowboy hat and put it over the speedometer. Cooed a reporter, "Mr. President, you're fun."

★ The president was really fun on some nights at the Lone Star State ranch. One White House secretary woke up at the spread to find LBJ climbing into bed with her. "Move over," he barked. "This is your president."

# John F. Kennedy
## All-American Presidential
## Bonus Chapter

### FACTS OF LIFE (and Death)

**ORIGIN:** Born John Fitzgerald Kennedy, May 29, 1917, Brookline, Massachusetts; assassinated November 22, 1963, Dallas, Texas.

**FORMATIVE YEARS:** Harvard College, B.S., 1940.

**FAMILY PLANNING:** Married (allegedly) Durie Malcolm (socialite), 1947; (allegedly) never divorced; married Jacqueline "Jackie" Lee Bouvier (reporter/socialite), September 12, 1953.

**SELECTED ELECTION SCORECARD:** 1946–50: won, U.S. House of Representatives, 11th District, Massachusetts. 1952–58: won, U.S. Senate, Massachusetts. 1960: won, U.S. president (assassinated November 22, 1963).

## QUICKIE BIO

*Camelot*, the musical based on the legend of King Arthur, is how America likes to recall the brief, glamorous presidency of John Fitzgerald Kennedy. *Guys and Dolls* might have been more appropriate, though no one could deny that President Kennedy came a lot. The third child of superrich liquor peddler, stock manipulator, movie mogul, and former ambassador Joseph Kennedy, JFK grew up in suburban Boston, New York, and Palm Beach. John prepped at Choate, dropped out of Princeton because of illness, and graduated from Harvard. During World War II, he served in the Navy aboard the boat *PT-109*, where he was wounded, later decorated, and earned the nickname "Shafty" for his onshore hijinks. After the war, Papa Joe declared, "We're going to sell Jack like soap flakes." With big money, savvy media manipulation, reddish brown hair, blue-gray eyes, and a sharp wit, Jack started his career as a fierce anti-Communist, and sped through the political food chain. In 1960 he beat Richard Nixon by the closest margin in history, to become America's youngest president. President Kennedy served his country, while relying on interns, call girls, aides, actresses, airline stewardesses, beauty queens, movie stars, and even his wife to satisfy his sexual needs. Nearly forty years after his tragic death, Americans still idolize the King of Camelot, and his reputation as a lothario has only added to his legacy. "It's not what you are that counts," JFK admitted, "but what people think you are."

## JOHN F. KENNEDY DOES
## THE DUMBEST THINGS

✪ Jack lost his virginity at seventeen in Harlem when he shared the same prostitute with a friend. Young Kennedy nicknamed his member "Lay More." After his circumcision, he called it "JJ."

✪ As a young Naval officer, Jack served at the Office of Naval Intelligence in Washington, D.C., and allegedly had an affair with a married reporter named Inga Arvad. He called her "Inga-Binga." She referred to him as "Honeysuckle." J. Edgar Hoover, head of the FBI, reportedly had tapes of Inga-Binga and Honeysuckle getting it on. When Jack's father Joe learned of the affair, he scolded Jack, then tried to seduce Inga-Binga himself.

✪ Jack and his crew were asleep on board *PT-109* in a combat zone when a Japanese destroyer ran into the boat and cut it in half. When asked how he became a World War II hero, Kennedy replied, "It was involuntary; they sank my boat."

✪ In 1946, newly elected Congressman Kennedy declared, "If you don't want to work for a living this is as good a job as any."

✪ In the early 1950s, Kennedy annoyed diners at a formal charity benefit in Newport, Rhode Island, when he disappeared into a coat closet with a good-looking woman. The guests waited impatiently for their coats while the young senator completed an in-depth discussion.

✪ Jack got tips on how to deal with women from friends like Bill Thompson, a railroad lobbyist and womanizer. One time, the two took the train to Miami accompanied by a few girls. Jack's mother Rose came to the station to meet the young men, but Jack couldn't find Bill. Kennedy finally knocked on the window of Bill's compartment. "I'm not ready to come out yet," Thompson boomed. "I've got one more girl to go."

✪ According to many of his sexual partners, Jack was a "wham-bam thank you ma'am" type of guy. The train pulled out of the station almost as quickly as it went in. Senator Kennedy liked to make love on the hardwood floor of his offices, and kept a picture of himself with several nude girls on the deck of a yacht on the desk in his Senate office.

✪ Jack lost the party's contest for vice president to Sen. Estes Kefauver (D-Tennessee) at the Democratic National Convention in 1956. The two rival candidates were intimately acquainted. Kefauver once attended a party at Jack's suite in the Mayflower Hotel in Washington. An FBI source reported that Jack and Estes, and "their respective dates made love in plain view of other partygoers. When they were done, the senators simply exchanged partners and began anew."

✪ "Ask not what your country can do for you," Kennedy declared in his inaugural address, "ask what you can do for your country . . ." JFK's speechwriter borrowed the phrase from another president who had declared, "Think more of what you can do for your government than of what your government can do for you." That president was Warren G. Harding.

✪ Jack realized there was a downside to being president. "I suppose if I win," he sighed, "my poon days are over."

✪ Not so! Journalists claimed that President JFK "ordered up prostitutes like most Americans sent out for sandwiches." Even as a senator, JFK usually didn't have to order in. Women sent notes to him saying things like, "Senator, you can put your shoes under my bed anytime you want."

★ While Jackie was recovering from the cesarean birth of her daughter Caroline, her sister Lee and her brother-in-law came to stay at the Kennedys' New York apartment. "Well, I am here in this apartment with Lee Bouvier," Jack joked. "If that isn't a test of character—which I have passed—nothing is." Not quite. Reportedly, one night Jack had sex with Lee while her husband listened in the next room. Lee later bragged about it to her friends.

★ Jack had an affair with staff aide Pamela Turnure. Turnure's landlady was a very religious woman who was outraged by the president's actions and photographed him coming out of Turnure's apartment. After he was elected president, Kennedy appointed Turnure as his wife Jackie's press secretary.

★ Jack Kennedy was sharp, animated, alert, and obviously knowledgeable during the 1960 televised presidential debate against Richard Nixon. Nixon looked like a scowling grumpmeister with a five-o'clock shadow. What was the Kennedy secret? Speed. Jack reportedly received injections of the drug from Dr. Max Jacobson, aka Dr. Feelgood, "the bat wing and chicken blood doctor," whose license to practice medicine was revoked fifteen years later.

★ Two young aides, blonde Priscilla Weir and brunette Jill Cowan, were known in the White House as Fiddle and Faddle. "It was common knowledge in the White House," a member of the staff confessed, "that when the president took lunch in the pool with Fiddle and Faddle, nobody goes in there." Except brothers Bobby and Teddy, who often joined big brother in his buck-naked romps.

★ Actress Jayne Mansfield claimed that she made love with JFK. The buxom blonde was eight months pregnant at the time and Kennedy was wearing a back brace. When Kennedy told Jayne that her voice reminded him of Jackie's she was insulted. "I don't sound like her. She doesn't sound like anything."

★ Kennedy family lore has it that Jackie once discovered women's underwear under her pillow at the White House. She held it out to the president, saying, "Would you please shop around and see who this belongs to? It's not my size."

★ According to one of Kennedy's Secret Service agents, Jack's sexual appetite was a bummer. "It caused a lot of morale problems. You were on the most elite assignment in the Secret Service, and you were there watching an elevator or a door because the president was inside with

"I was Frank's [Sinatra] pimp and Frank was Jack's [John Kennedy]," claimed Peter Lawford (right), who married JFK's sister and liked to hang out with the president (left). "It sounds terrible now, but then it was really a lot of fun."
(Courtesy of John F. Kennedy Library)

two hookers." The Secret Service often joked that they couldn't protect the president from getting a venereal disease.

⭐ Kennedy did contract a venereal disease, chlamydia. And like Bob Dole, Kennedy required treatment for occasional erectile dysfunction.

⭐ President Kennedy knew how to take care of business. One day, he was having sex in the Lincoln bedroom of the White House when he heard a knock on the door. The president got out of bed, and flung open the door. Two male advisors came into the room and handed Kennedy a classified cable. He sat down on a chair, read the message, and made a decision while his naked female partner looked on from the bed.

⭐ JFK's brother-in-law was actor Peter Lawford, one of the members of the Hollywood Rat Pack. Peter introduced Jack to Frank Sinatra, the founder and leader of the Rat Pack. Frank, in turn, introduced Jack to a woman named Judith Campbell. Campbell, who was born Judith Immoor and later married professional golfer Dan Exner, claimed that she had an affair with Jack in 1960. Campbell insisted she was also having an affair with Chicago gangster Sam Giancana at the same time.

Not only was Judith supposedly having sexual encounters with the president, she was also purportedly shuttling satchels of money between JFK and "Momo" Giancana to cover up voter fraud in the 1960 election. Campbell claimed that when she complained of FBI harassment, the president responded, "You have nothing to be afraid of. . . . You know Sam works for us."

★ The Kennedy entourage had a blast at Bing Crosby's estate in Palm Springs, California. One Secret Service man recalled a pool party at Crosby's pad two months after the Cuban missile crisis. The agent remembers seeing one aide "banging a girl on the edge of the pool. The president is sitting across the pool, having a drink and talking to some broads. Everybody was buckass-naked."

★ Later, Kennedy's aide started bringing Crosby's suits out of his house and throwing them into the pool. According to the Secret Service dude, JFK "thought that was pretty funny—laughed and nearly fell out of his chair." When Bing returned home, he, however, didn't think it was funny. The White House, apparently at taxpayers' expense, paid for the damaged suits.

★ Several months later, JFK returned to Crosby's Palm Springs manse. He made a pass at a girl, accidentally fell into the pool, and injured his back. As a result, he had to wear a rigid back brace, which he was still wearing the day he was assassinated.

★ Another one of Peter Lawford's bosom buddies was Marilyn Monroe. Jack was introduced to the actress in 1954, and met with her numerous times at Lawford's place in 1957 and 1959. In her biography entitled *Bitch!—The Autobiography of Lady Lawford as Told to Buddy Galon* (1986), Lawford's mother, Lady May, sighed, "I find it difficult to place my complete trust in a president of the United States who always had his mind on his c**k!"

★ During the Democratic National Convention in 1960, Kennedy dated Marilyn and stuck his hand up her dress. Later, Monroe commented that his performance had been "very democratic" and "very penetrating" and went nude swimming with Jack after he gave his acceptance speech.

★ The day after winning the Democratic nomination, Jack, Marilyn Monroe, and actress Jeanne Carmen attended a wild party at Peter Lawford's house. Kennedy supposedly suggested a three-way sexual encounter with Marilyn and Jeanne. Carmen declined, but Marilyn reportedly tried to convince her by saying, "We can think of it as helping out the country." Then Jack is purported to have said, "Just think of it as standing on the edge of a New Frontier, the frontier of the 1960s. A frontier of unknown opportunities and perils. Jeanne, I'm asking you and Marilyn both to be new pioneers on that New Frontier."

✪ In May 1962, Marilyn defied her Hollywood bosses and traveled to New York City's Madison Square Garden to perform for JFK's forty-fifth birthday bash. Monroe wore a $12,000 beaded gown that she had to be sewn into, then took the stage and sang "Happy Birthday" to the president. The chief executive said privately, "What an a**. . . . What an a**." In public he declared, "I can now retire from politics after having 'Happy Birthday' sung to me in such a sweet, wholesome way."

✪ Not long after Marilyn's birthday serenade, Jack Kennedy's brother Bobby visited the movie star and told her that the president was breaking off their affair. Then Bobby reportedly bedded the blonde star himself. After both Kennedy brothers dumped her, Marilyn tried frantically to call the White House but was unable to get through. She died on August 5, 1962, in Los Angeles, an apparent suicide.

✪ Speech writer Ted Sorensen joked, "This administration is going to do for sex what the last one [Dwight Eisenhower's] did for golf." Kennedy shot back, "You mean nineteen holes in one day?"

✪ When JFK learned of a CIA plan to oust Cuba's communist dictator Fidel Castro, the president observed, "You always assume that the military and intelligence people have some secret skill not available to ordinary mortals." Kennedy approved the plan. In April 1961, the CIA arranged the landing of 1,400 American-trained Cuban soldiers on a stretch of supposedly deserted beach in Cuba. The beach turned out to be one of Castro's favorite fishing spots. The troops were captured and four American fliers were killed in the Bay of Pigs fiasco. Looking back, Kennedy complained, "All my life, I've known better than to depend on the experts. How could I have been so stupid. . . ."

✪ After the Bay of Pigs disaster, Kennedy's approval rating went up to 82 percent. "My God, it's as bad as Eisenhower," Kennedy sighed. "The worse I do, the more popular I get."

✪ Eleven days after the Bay of Pigs, JFK's men started Operation Mongoose. It was an effort to oust Castro by any means necessary. Methods that were considered included poison pills and exploding cigars.

✪ After the Bay of Pigs mess, the Soviets deployed missiles on Cuba. For thirteen days, the United States and Russia faced off while Kennedy demanded that the missiles be removed from Cuba. The Soviets backed down eventually, but during the crisis, Kennedy noticed a cute new secretary. "I want her name and number," the president demanded. "We may avert war here tonight."

✪ Kennedy's brain trust—dubbed "the best and brightest"—not only approved of the Bay of Pigs, they masterminded the escalation of the war in Vietnam. "I don't think the intelligence reports are all that hot," Jack sighed. "Some days I get more out of the *New York Times.*"

✪ At the Berlin Wall in West Berlin, Kennedy said, "*Ich bin ein Berliner,*" which means, "I am a cream-filled pastry." What Kennedy meant to say was, "*Ich bin Berliner,*" which means, "I am a citizen of Berlin."

✪ Over the Labor Day weekend in 1963, Jack thought it would be fun to make a home movie. He decided to film his own execution. A Navy photographer filmed Jack getting off the presidential yacht, clutching his chest, and falling down. A beautiful young woman stepped over him with her son, then Jackie, then a buddy stumbled on him, and red liquid spurted from Jack's mouth onto his shirt.

✪ After his national funeral in Washington, D.C., President Kennedy was buried at Arlington National Cemetery in Virginia, across the Potomac River from Washington, D.C. Jackie hired a well-known architect to design the memorial. She knew the architect so well that she allegedly had a two-year affair with him while he was creating the special tribute.

# Teddy Kennedy

## FACTS OF LIFE

**ORIGIN:** Born Edward Moore Kennedy, February 22, 1932, Boston, Massachusetts.

**FORMATIVE YEARS:** Harvard University, A.B., 1954; The International Law School, 1958; University of Virginia, LL.B., 1959.

**FAMILY PLANNING:** Married Virginia Joan Bennett (model/queen of the Bermuda Floral Pageant), November 29, 1958; divorced, 1982; married Victoria Reggie (lawyer), July 3, 1992.

**SELECTED ELECTION SCORECARD:** 1962: won, U.S. Senate, Massachusetts (elected to fill the vacancy caused by the resignation of his brother John F. Kennedy). 1964–94: won, U.S. Senate, Massachusetts.

## QUICKIE BIO

Described by his brother JFK as "the gay illiterate," and dubbed by a journalist "a fathead," Teddy Kennedy had the longest, and most scandalous, political career of any Kennedy. The youngest son of Joe and Rose Kennedy, Teddy took his first communion from the hands of Pope Pius XII, and headed off to boarding school at age eight. Over the next five years he attended ten different boarding and day schools. He managed to make it through Harvard as an undergraduate, but couldn't get into Harvard Law School, and worked as a reporter before earning his law degree in 1959.

Kennedy worked on his big brother's political campaign, and took Jack's U.S. Senate seat in 1962. He sat there for the next thirty-eight years, becoming one of the most powerful liberal politicians in America. But Kennedy's legacy has less to do with legislation than with partying. In July 1969, Teddy further opened up the private lives of politicians to journalistic investigation when he had a car accident on Chappaquiddick Island, off the coast of Martha's Vineyard in Massachusetts. But what can you expect from a man who was described by one of his congressional colleagues as "the least discreet guy on the Hill"? "Oh, Teddy and his girls," his mom, Rose Kennedy, complained once. "What can a mother do?"

## TEDDY KENNEDY DOES THE DUMBEST THINGS

⭐ Teddy was cited for reckless driving three times in 1958, and once in 1959, and earned the nickname "Cadillac Eddie."

⭐ On a cruise from Cape Cod to Maine, Ted was taunted by the crew of another yacht. He got so angry that he leaped off his boat, jumped on board the other yacht, and threw eight people into the water.

⭐ Ted reportedly hired a substitute to take a Spanish exam for him while he was a student at Harvard. Unfortunately, the phony Ted was nabbed when he handed in the test. Both students were expelled from school, but later readmitted.

⭐ After leaving Harvard, Teddy enlisted in the Army. He thought he had signed up for two years, but had actually committed to four. His father fumed, "Don't you ever look at what you're signing?" Joe Kennedy then arranged for his son's enlistment to be shortened. Teddy never rose above the rank of private.

⭐ While working on his brother's presidential campaign, Ted took in Frank Sinatra's show at the Sands Casino in Las Vegas, and was introduced to Judith Campbell. Ted sat next to her, but when he tried to get into her room, she put him off by saying, "I know you don't want me to lose my patience." He laughed, "Oh, God, no. That's the last thing I want you to lose." Apparently, Teddy didn't realize that Judith was already going out with his brother Jack.

⭐ In the spring of 1969, Teddy began drinking from a flask that had been his brother Bobby's and shouted, "They're going to shoot my a** off the way they shot Bobby's." Another time, on a plane in Alaska, a drunken Teddy walked up and down the aisle chanting, "Eskimo Pow-er, Eskimo Pow-eeerr!"

⭐ On the night of July 18, 1969, Ted Kennedy partied with several "boiler-room girls" from his deceased brother Bobby's presidential campaign, then borrowed a 1967 Oldsmobile sedan, jumped into the car with twenty-eight-year-old Mary Jo Kopechne, and, shortly after, drove off a bridge and into a tidal pool on Chappaquiddick Island, Massachusetts. The car sank and Mary Jo drowned. Teddy wound up at a hotel in Edgartown on Martha's Vineyard, where he rested and made seventeen phone calls. He didn't report the incident to police until after it was discovered—ten hours after it had occurred.

⭐ Many years later, in October 1991, Kennedy was on the panel that heard law professor Anita Hill testify about U.S. Supreme Court Justice nominee Clarence Thomas. Hill testified that Thomas had talked about porn star "Long Dong Silver," boasted about the size of his own penis, and held up a Coke can proclaiming, "Who put pubic hair in my Coke?" After Hill's testimony, Kennedy declared indignantly, "Are we an old-boys club—insensitive at best, and perhaps something worse?"

⭐ Sen. Orrin Hatch (R-Utah) once replied to a rhetorical question by Ted: "Anybody who believes that, I know a bridge up in Massachusetts that I'll be happy to sell them on behalf of the senator from Massachusetts."

"The blonde-of-the-week-club." That's what Washington insiders called Suzy "Suzy Chapstick" Chaffee, the "T-shirt girl," and the numerous other blondes who "befriended" Sen. Teddy Kennedy during the 1980s. In 1994 the blonde First Lady Hillary Clinton taught the aging Kennedy some new tricks.
(Courtesy of Reuters/Jim Bourg/ Archive Photos)

Hatch later apologized for his "unfortunate and insensitive mistake," and asked that "a bridge in Brooklyn" be substituted in the record. Hatch later wrote and recorded a love song for Teddy and his second wife Vicki entitled, "Souls Along the Way."

★ After losing the 1980 Democratic presidential primary, Kennedy allegedly drowned his sorrows in a mountain of cocaine. His aides recalled that he showed up at his Senate office with "watery eyes and sore nostrils," and some supposedly reported that the senator had white powder clinging to his nose.

★ By the late 1980s writers were saying, "I think he's mad," and, "He's off the reservation." In 1989, a bouncer recalled Kennedy appearing at a bar in New York City at 1:00 A.M., "absolutely inebriated." When a patron said, "You're nothing like your brothers," Kennedy threw a drink in his face. A few hours later, some friends hauled him out of the joint and loaded the senator into a cab. Appropriately enough, the name of the bar was American Trash.

★ One woman recalled the senator's pickup technique: "It was pathetic, very high-school, a lot of giggling and heavy breathing."

★ In 1987, Teddy had lunch with a young blonde lobbyist. Then the senator decided to have dessert. A waitress came in and supposedly found Kennedy on the floor with his pants off, on top of the lobbyist.

★ Kennedy was photographed on top of a twenty-two-year-old woman, on a speed boat owned by game-show producer Chuck Barris. While examining the photo, Sen. Howell Heflin (D-Alabama) declared, "Well, Teddy, I see you've changed your position on offshore drilling."

★ In 1993, the senator attended his annual Christmas bash dressed like Barney the Dinosaur, and performed in a skit in which he joked, "They don't call me 'Tyrannosaurus Sex' for nothing."

# Those Other Kennedys

## QUICKIE PROFILE

They started out as two in 1914—Joe and Rose Kennedy. However, by the year 2000, there were more than five dozen Kennedy descendants and in-laws running around the country, getting into telephone communications, oil, magazines, and, yes, unfortunately, politics. Old Joe tried hard to set things up for his fertile dynasty. He made money in banking, booze, stocks, and movies. According to some critics, he accumulated money the old-fashioned way—illegally. Mobster Sam Giancana called Joe "one of the biggest crooks who ever lived." Crooked or not, Joe set up large trust funds for his wife and nine kids. Too bad. With the trusts out of their control and conveniently paying their bills, the Kennedys were able to indulge in huge amounts of dumb stuff over the decades. In total the Kennedys founded more than a dozen non-profit organizations, and spent quality time at fourteen different drug-rehab facilities. In all fairness, the Kennedy women have been a bit more reasonable than the men. Nevertheless, on the whole, the Kennedy clan has evolved into the head lice of American politics—numerous, annoying, and seemingly impossible to get rid of. Yet sometimes they get rid of themselves.

## OTHER KENNEDYS DO
## THE DUMBEST THINGS

### JOSEPH PATRICK KENNEDY (born 1888; died 1969)

⭐ Joe's father owned a bar in Boston, Massachusetts. One of Joe's earliest memories was of two of his dad's pals coming to the house and bragging that they had each cast 128 votes that day.

⭐ In 1926 Joe got into the film business and founded what was eventually to become RKO Pictures. He specialized in making low-budget films and wooing high-profile actresses. Joe invited screen siren Gloria Swanson and her husband to his mansion in Palm Beach, Florida. After he sent Gloria's spouse out fishing, Joe pounced on the actress. According to Swanson, "He stroked my body and pulled at my kimono. He kept insisting in a drawn-out moan, 'No longer, no longer. Now.' He was like a roped horse, rough, arduous, racing to be free. After a hasty climax he lay beside me, stroking my hair. Apart from his guilty, passionate mutterings, he still said nothing cogent."

⭐ Joe laid out pornographic magazines for his fourteen-year-old son Jack to study.

⭐ Joe shared with his children his passion for politics. He also shared girlfriends with them. Screen legend Marlene Dietrich claimed she had slept with Joe Senior, Joe Jr., and Jack.

⭐ Late one night at the Kennedy home, a friend of Joe's daughter was in one of the guest bedrooms sleeping. She awoke to find Joe next to her, taking off his robe. Joe said, "This is going to be something you'll always remember."

⭐ Pres. Franklin Roosevelt appointed Joe as the U.S. Ambassador to the Court of St. James, making him the American government's representative in London. Barbara Hutton, the Woolworth heiress, went to Joe's office. First he agreed to arrange for her to return to America even though she had renounced her citizenship. Then Kennedy began to flirt with her and chased her around his desk.

⭐ Kennedy was aggressive with women, but not against the Nazis. He told anyone who would listen that Britain was going to lose the war against Germany, and that America should not get involved in any conflict in Europe.

# ROBERT "BOBBY" FRANCIS KENNEDY (born 1925; assassinated 1968)

✪ While managing his brother John's campaign for the U.S. Senate in 1952, Robert Kennedy declared, "I don't want my brother to get mixed up with politicians."

✪ While he was the U.S. Attorney General in his brother's Presidency, Bobby went to a nude beach with Marilyn Monroe and actress Jeanne Carmen. Bobby wore a fake beard, a cap, and sunglasses. He giggled, "I can't believe I'm doing this! I just can't believe it!"

# JACQUELINE "JACKIE" BOUVIER KENNEDY (wife of John Fitzgerald Kennedy; born 1929; died 1994)

✪ Jacqueline's father was John Vernon "Black Jack" Bouvier III, a notorious womanizer, who bragged to Jackie about bedding tobacco heiress Doris Duke during his honeymoon cruise with Jackie's mother. When a friend tried to talk Jackie out of marrying Jack Kennedy, she admitted that she expected him to be unfaithful, just like her dad had been.

✪ Jackie played around a bit herself. In August 1962, she hung out with Gianni Agnelli, heir to the Fiat car fortune. A CIA official later told the story of the agency receiving a call from Jackie asking them to fetch her diaphragm and send it by the next plane to Ravello, Italy, where she was partying with Gianni.

✪ Jackie married Greek shipping magnate Aristotle Onassis on October 20, 1968. He was shorter and twelve years older than she was, but an awful lot richer. By 1970 Onassis was back with his mistress, opera diva Maria Callas. Later, he complained to his lawyer, "The marriage has gotten down to a monthly presentation of bills."

# JOHN "JOHN-JOHN" F. KENNEDY JR. (son of John Fitzgerald Kennedy; born 1960; died 1999, in a plane crash with his wife and sister-in-law while he was piloting)

✪ John Jr. flunked the New York State Bar twice and declared, "I'm clearly not a major legal genius."

✪ John Jr. went out with several actresses including Daryl Hannah, Madonna, and Christina Haag. He appeared onstage acting in a play opposite Haag. At the end of the play, they both drowned, which ironically, is exactly what happened to him in real life in the plane crash of 1999.

✪ John Jr. founded the magazine *George* in 1995. In one issue he called his cousins "poster boys for bad behavior," and posed nude. His cousin

Joseph P. Kennedy II responded with, "Ask not what you can do for your cousin, but what you can do for his magazine."

# REP. JOSEPH PATRICK KENNEDY II (D-MASSACHUSETTS)
(son of Robert Francis Kennedy; born 1952)

⭐ On his résumé, Joe listed, "1974 Peace Corps volunteer—Kenya (assisted in the development of an agricultural project)." When challenged about his Peace Corps experience, Kennedy's office clarified the entry, explaining that Joe had not actually been a Peace Corps volunteer. He was in Kenya roping giraffes for a TV program when he helped out a Peace Corps project.

⭐ In 1973 Joe followed in the tracks of his uncle Teddy and got into car trouble. Joe drove a Jeep offroad, doing wild turns around trees until he wrecked the vehicle. He was unhurt, but a female passenger was left paralyzed from the waist down, and David, Joe's younger brother, suffered fractured vertebrae.

⭐ Sometimes Joe overestimated the clout of the Kennedy name. When the counter help at a bakery told Joe the store didn't take checks, Joe screamed back, "Don't you know who I am?"

⭐ Joe divorced his wife Sheila Rauch Kennedy to wed Anne Elizabeth "Beth" Kelly, a member of his staff. But Kennedy couldn't get the Catholic Church to grant him an annulment of his first union, so he married in a civil ceremony. Later, Kennedy was granted an annulment. His first spouse was furious, but Joe explained to her that it was "just Catholic gobbledygook."

# ROBERT F. KENNEDY JR. (son of Robert Francis Kennedy; born 1954)

⭐ On a plane flight in September 1983, Robert F. Kennedy Jr. went into the restroom and didn't come out. Attendants found him sitting on the toilet mumbling incoherently. He seemed to be in withdrawal from heroin. They checked his bags, reportedly found drugs, and detained him.

⭐ Robert Jr. worked for the New York City District Attorney's Office. While prosecuting one assault case, he fell asleep in court.

⭐ While traveling in Peru in South America, Bobby Jr. climbed out the window of a moving bus to get a sweater out of his duffel bag on the roof.

⭐ Bobby sold his brother David a pound of pot but the marijuana got stolen at David's school. So Bobby went to the school disguised as a tough drug dealer and threatened the other students. One youngster went to the faculty, who threw David out of the school.

## DAVID ANTHONY KENNEDY (son of Robert Francis Kennedy; born 1955; died 1984, of a drug overdose)

✪ In September 1975, David was beaten and robbed of $30 in a Harlem hotel. David reported that two men had waved down his BMW and stolen his money at knifepoint. Actually David was probably trying to score drugs. The hotel in which he was assaulted was a drug shooting gallery. Supposedly, the regulars knew David as "White James" and "Sweetwater."

✪ In 1978, David Kennedy asked to spend time at the family compound in Hyannisport, Massachusetts, and told his uncle Teddy, "I promise to be a good boy." A short time later, good boy David phoned Supreme Court Justice William O. Douglas to report a burglary. When investigators arrived, they reportedly found David and his girlfriend passed out in the house, the window broken, and the room in shambles with blood, needles, and vials strewn all around. There had been no burglary. Apparently David had just flipped out.

✪ After trashing his house in Hyannisport, David went to uncle Teddy's place in McLean, Virginia, took a credit card, and explained to the servants, "My uncle's as bad as I am; he can't do anything for me."

## WILLIAM KENNEDY SMITH (son of Jean Ann Kennedy; born 1960)

✪ In March 1991, Willie went to Palm Beach, Florida, with his uncle Teddy and his cousin Patrick, who later was elected to the U.S. House of Representatives from Rhode Island. Teddy later described it as a "typical Easter weekend." At 11:30 P.M., Senator Ted woke up Willie and Patrick and talked them into joining him for a few beers at a local nightclub. Reportedly, Willie picked up a girl, Patty Bowman, at the bar. Teddy and Patrick left at 2:00 A.M. Willie stayed and then got a ride home with Patty. He walked with her to the beach, stripped, and went into the surf. When they walked to the pool, Willie stripped again. She alleged that he wrestled her to the ground and supposedly raped her. He claimed she allowed him to have sex with her. One thing they both agreed on. During the act, Willie kept calling Patty "Kathy."

✪ Willie was tried for rape. Two other women came forward to claim that he had attacked them once. Their testimony was not allowed in court, and Willie was found not guilty.

✪ Although William Kennedy Smith got off free, his reputation followed him. In October 1993, Willie was at a bar in Virginia. A patron reportedly yelled out, "Hey, it's Willie the rapist!" Then another guy shouted, "You got lucky, Willie," and sat down with Willie and his date. When Willie started shoving the guy, a large bouncer escorted Willie out. Smith smacked the bouncer with a punch in the face. The man hit Willie back. According to the bartender, "He [Willie] suddenly turned from a human being into an animal."

## MICHAEL LEMOYNE KENNEDY (son of Robert Francis Kennedy; born 1958; died 1998 after skiing into a tree at Aspen, Colorado)

✪ As a kid Michael often answered the phone with, "Confusion here."

✪ Michael married gridiron star Frank Gifford's daughter Victoria. Then he had an affair with his babysitter, beginning when she was fourteen years old. Kennedy didn't deny the affair, but claimed that it had started when the babysitter was sixteen years old. Wife Victoria split after she reportedly caught Michael and the hired help in bed together.

✪ The Kennedys were famous for their holiday touch-football games. In January 1998, Michael and his family began playing touch football on the ski slopes at Aspen. Oops! Michael skied into a tree and died.

# Ed Koch

## FACTS OF LIFE

**ORIGIN:** Born Edward Irving Koch, December 12, 1924, Bronx, New York.

**FORMATIVE YEARS:** Attended City College of New York; New York University Law School, LL.B., 1948.

**FAMILY PLANNING:** Unmarried.

**SELECTED ELECTION SCORECARD:** 1968–76: won, U.S. House of Representatives, 17th District, New York. 1977–85: won, mayor, New York City.

## QUICKIE BIO

You'd think only a schmuck would want to be mayor of New York City, when black citizens heckle you with, "Don't let him speak. Send the Jew back to the synagogues!" But Ed Koch was a mensch who was just as loud and obnoxious as his constituents. A confirmed bachelor who liked to relax in his rent-controlled Greenwich Village apartment even when he lived in the mayor's baronial Gracie Mansion, Koch got his start in the "club" political system that once ruled the Big Apple. He served in the U.S. House of Representatives, but didn't make headlines until he became mayor of New York City. Ed consistently denied rumors that he was gay, swore never to wear a toupee, and admitted that he did not walk through Central Park at night because "that's just tempting fate." By the end of his third term, Koch's self-promoting style made him seem like New York's chief eccentric. So whaddaya think he did? He got into "entahtainment." He worked as a radio talk-show guy and as a TV judge. What else is a tall bald retired Jewish politician from Brooklyn gonna do? Sing in Nashville? Git outta heah, you wacko.

# ED KOCH DOES
# THE DUMBEST THINGS

⭐ In his first race for the mayoralty of New York City, Koch faced off against Mario Cuomo. Cuomo's people accused Koch campaigners of driving a truck around and announcing from a loudspeaker, "A vote for Cuomo is a vote for the Mafia." A Cuomo enthusiast supposedly put up posters that read, "Vote for Cuomo, not the homo."

⭐ Mayor Koch appeared on a call-in radio show in the early 1980s. A caller complained, "I was passing a theater on the block and I looked in the window and there was a two-hundred-and-fifty-pound naked lady cooking in the window. I find that objectionable." Mayor Koch ordered an investigation of the naked fat lady. The findings? The female was indeed naked and was indeed fat, but she was also a member of the Squat Theater. "The woman has been described as an authentic American witch who acts out a real witch's ceremony in the window," the report detailed. "This play, supported with a grant from the New York State Council on the Arts, was apparently very popular." Mayor Koch carried a copy of the report with him, and often read from it to get laughs.

⭐ When Ed Koch ordered organizations in New York City to pay their outstanding water bills, he encountered great opposition. Addressing a group representing colleges and universities, Koch said, "If you don't want to pay, don't drink. But if you drink, you pay. Listen, you know what I said to Yeshiva University? 'You don't want to pay? Close your mikvahs!' " Mikvahs are Jewish ritual baths.

⭐ During a strike of New York City transportation workers in 1979, a protester approached Koch in the rain, yelling, "You strikebreaker!" "You know," Koch told the press, "the wackos apparently don't come out in the rain. Only one."

⭐ In the summer of 1982, Ed suggested sending Pres. Ronald Reagan to China. "Ronald Reagan will commit hara-kiri [Japanese ritual suicide]," the mayor predicted, because he "has hoof-in-mouth disease."

⭐ Waiters reported in 1981 that Ed Koch was eating pork at a Chinese restaurant in New York City, when he began to choke and was rescued with the Heimlich maneuver. Later, the Jewish Koch claimed that he had choked on sautéed watercress, not on the ritually forbidden pork.

⭐ Koch welcomed a group of Soviet children to the Big Apple, then told them that their government was "the pits." One of the youths complained, "I want to get on the bus and go far away from this place."

"I pledge to you that if Israel ever invades the United States, I shall stand with the United States," declared Ed Koch, standing here next to 8-foot-3-inch-tall Muhammad Alam Channa, the tallest man in the world.
(Courtesy of AP/World Wide Photos)

✪ Ed appointed his good pal Bess Myerson to be Cultural Affairs Commissioner of New York City. Oops! Myerson, who in 1945 became the first Jewish woman to become Miss America and who later became a popular TV personality, was once detained for alleged shoplifting in London. She was held again in Pennsylvania for supposedly stealing $44.07 worth of batteries, earrings, nail polish, and shoes. Then, later, there were the indictments on charges of bribery, conspiracy, and mail fraud.

✪ The ultimate New Yorker, Koch once told *Playboy* magazine that residing in rural areas was a "joke." He then described living in the New York State capital of Albany as "a fate worse than death." Then he ran for governor of New York—and lost.

✪ At one time Ed Koch was quoted on the subject of reincarnation, "I want to come back as me."

# Lyndon LaRouche

## FACTS OF LIFE

**ORiGiN:** Born Lyndon H. LaRouche Jr., September 8, 1922, Rochester, New Hampshire.

**FORMATiVE YEARS:** Raised as a Quaker; joined the Communist Party in Calcutta, India.

**FAMiLY PLANNiNG:** Married Janice (common-law wife); divorced, 1970s; married Helga Zepp (devoted LaRouche follower), 1977.

**SELECTED ELECTiON SCORECARD:** 1976–96: lost, U.S. president; 2000: potential candidate for U.S. president.

## QUICKIE BIO

The FBI. Russia's KGB. Colombian drug lords. The royal family of England. They were all out to get Lyndon LaRouche, or so the perennial Democratic political loser liked to imagine. Actually, LaRouche seemed to be the most paranoid Democrat in American history, a man who was a conspiracy junkie before such things were cool. LaRouche joined the Trotskyite Socialist Workers Party in 1948, but really jumped into politics in the 1960s when he

93

became a Marxist beatnik in New York City's Greenwich Village, and the organizer of a far-left political fringe group. Then, like Ronald Reagan, LaRouche veered dramatically from far left to far right. Unlike Reagan, LaRouche had no apparent political savvy and no sense of humor. Many would claim that he had no sense at all. His organization was described as "one of the most bizarre cults in the history of the United States." LaRouche lectured his followers that the world was on the verge of destruction, involving a vast conspiracy between the IMF (International Monetary Fund), AIDS (the disease), and the phone cartel. What inspired LaRouche to lead the far-right fringe of the Democratic Party? Many people believe that Lyndon went right when his first wife left him for a leftist. After that happened, LaRouche liked to spend long hours sitting in his apartment with stockpiles of canned food and guards at the door. At least running for president got him out of the house.

## LYNDON LAROUCHE DOES
## THE DUMBEST THINGS

✪ In April 1973, LaRouche organized Operation Mop-Up. The group mopped up by breaking up meetings of communists across the U.S. How did they do it? By busting into the gatherings, brawling with the communists, and throwing chairs around. Operation Mop-Up resulted in many injuries, a few arrests, and no convictions.

✪ During his 1984 presidential campaign, LaRouche ran with slogans like "Nuclear Power Is Safer than Sex" and "Feed Jane Fonda to the Whales." LaRouche also declared that the birthmark on the head of Soviet leader Mikhail Gorbachev was the sign of Satan.

✪ In 1984, LaRouche supporter Debra Freeman ran against Rep. Barbara Mikulski (D-Maryland) in the Democratic primary in that state. Freeman's ads labeled Mikulski "the beast of Baltimore." "We haven't heard a lot from Barbara," the radio ads declared, "but when we have heard from her it has sounded like this." What followed was the sound of monkeys, baboons, and hyenas.

✪ Two years later, LaRouche followers Mark Fairchild and Janice Hart won the Democratic nominations for lieutenant governor and secretary of the state of Illinois. At a victory press conference, Hart told reporters, "We're going to roll our tanks down State Street." Adlai Stevenson III, the Democratic nominee for governor, declared that he would withdraw from the Democratic ticket rather than run with the LaRouche gang. Janice Hart called Stevenson a "wimp."

★ Janice Hart once accused Milwaukee Catholic archbishop Rembert Weakland of supporting the International Monetary Fund. Hart protested during a lecture by Weakland, and handed the cleric a piece of raw liver, calling it "a pound of flesh." Called into court for her actions, she refused to appear and claimed that she was in West Germany "campaigning for patriots."

★ For some years LaRouche raised money by selling publications at airports. Sales were meager, but he raised additional funds by encouraging customers to use credit cards and purportedly overbilling them. Followers justified their actions because they believed they were following a "higher law" and that the continued existence of the human race depended on supporting LaRouche.

★ Eventually Lyndon was convicted of conspiracy to defraud the Internal Revenue Service and of mail fraud in 1988, and was sent to prison. But that didn't keep him from running for president from his prison cell in 1992.

★ A LaRouche supporter ran as a Democrat against Rep. John Shadegg (R-Arizona) in 1996. Referring to a horrible airline crash, she dubbed Shadegg "Congressman ValuJet," who wished to "send your Social Security crashing into the Everglades swamps." As ValuJet Airlines explored legal action, the right-wing Democrat offended Jewish groups by saying that Shadegg wanted "to push your parents into the gas ovens of managed care." The head of the Arizona Democratic Party tried to convince the LaRouche supporter to tone down her campaign language, but explained, "This is a woman who has sued me and called me a 'Gingrichite Democrat,' so I am probably not the first person she goes to for political advice."

★ LaRouche ran for president in 2000, as he had done six times before. Unlike most candidates, however, LaRouche almost never appeared in public. Why? "If I walk out on the streets like a normal person," Lyndon explained, "I'm dead in a week."

# Local Loonies

## Wacky Way-Out
## Bonus Chapter

### DUMBEST QUOTES

"Give us this day our daily bread and forgive us our trespasses—get that son of a bitch, he's stealing my coat—as we forgive those who trespass against us . . ."
(Rep. James Michael Curley [D-Massachusetts],
running for mayor of Boston in 1914)

"The streets are safe in Philadelphia,
it's only the people who make them unsafe."
(Frank Rizzo, mayor of Philadelphia)

"I'm gonna be so tough as mayor I'm gonna
make Attila the Hun look like a faggot."
(Frank Rizzo, mayor of Philadelphia)

"Those who survived the San Francisco earthquake said,
'Thank God, I'm still alive.' But, of course, those who
died, their lives will never be the same again."
(U.S. Rep. Barbara Boxer [D-California])

"Women prefer Democrats to men."
(U.S. Rep. Tony Coehlo [D-California])

"I think the free-enterprise system is
absolutely too important to be left to the
voluntary action of the marketplace."
(U.S. Rep. Richard Kelly [D-Florida])

> "The first black president will be a
> politician who is black."
> **(Gov. Doug Wilder [D-Virginia])**
>
> "He may be a human jackal. He may be a son of the
> devil, although to call this aggregation of insolence,
> this consummate image of depravity who moves
> about the sacred chambers of our legislative halls
> with moral putrefaction oozing from his hide,
> a child of the devil would be to wrong the devil."
> **(Rep. James Harvey "Cyclone" Davis [D-Texas],**
> **who served in Congress from 1915–17)**

## LOCAL LOONIES PROFILE

Watch out! There are hundreds of thousands of them out there at this very minute—elected officials doing incredibly dumb things. You can find them in the sheriff's office, in the county courthouse, in city hall, in the courtrooms, in the great rotundas of the state capitol buildings, yes, even in the halls of the U.S. House of Representatives, the U.S. Senate, and in the basement of the White House. Most of these men and women will make a name for themselves by doing one or two incredibly dumb things, and then disappear from public view. Although they may not have had the longevity of the Democrats discussed elsewhere in this book, their actions deserve recognition as among the dumbest on record. Below is an honor roll of those local loonies who deserve special recognition. Do you know of any local Democrats who might fit into this chapter? Do you have a published account to prove it? Then contact us on the Internet at politicians@dumbest.com. Your country will thank you, especially the Republicans.

## LOCAL LOONIES DO
## THE DUMBEST THINGS

# MAYOR WILLIE L. BROWN JR. (D-California)

✪ "Street lights, dog doo, and parking meters are not my cup of tea," declared longtime Speaker of the California State House of Representatives Willie Brown. He later changed his mind and decided to run for mayor of San Francisco.

⭐ In 1995, Brown campaigned for mayor of the Golden Gate City against Frank Jordan, the former chief of police. During the contest, Jordan tried to loosen up his image. How did he do it? By posing for photographers while he was standing nude in a shower with two male disc jockeys. Brown won.

⭐ After the 49ers lost to the Dallas Cowboys, Mayor Brown called 49ers quarterback Elvis Grbac "an embarrassment to humankind," then flew off on a private plane to party in Paris. Later Grbac revealed that he was distracted during the game because his son was undergoing spinal surgery for a birth defect. Brown apologized saying, "It was a dumb thing to have uttered."

## KENDALL B. COFFEY (D-Florida)

⭐ As the U.S. Attorney for the Southern District of Florida, Coffey was prosecuting two drug lords. He was so sure of the case that he turned down a plea bargain in which the defendants were willing to forfeit more than $20 million to the U.S. government. But the jury acquitted the drug dealers. After his dramatic courtroom loss, Kendall drowned his sorrows at a gentleman's club, supposedly bit a topless dancer on the arm, and resigned his government post.

## REP. MARTIN DIES JR. (D-Texas)

⭐ In March 1954, terrorists stood up in the visitors' gallery of the U.S. House of Representatives, shouted, "Free Puerto Rico!" and began shooting at the members of the House. Five congressmen were hit by bullets while others ran for cover. Two overweight congressmen, Frank Boykin (D-Alabama) and Martin Dies, tried to escape through the same door at the same time and got stuck. Later, when the House discussed new security measures, Dies declared, "The safety measure most needed around here is bigger doors!"

⭐ In 1938, Dies was appointed as the first chairman of the House Un-American Activities Committee. Dies's committee was so vigilant in rooting out commies that it questioned the loyalty of Christopher Marlowe, an English playwright who lived in the 1500s, and launched an investigation of the hair tonic Kreml, because of the similarity between its brand name and the hated Kremlin. Dies also named as Communists the entire football and basketball teams of an El Paso, Texas, high school, whom the local constabulary suspected of being revolutionaries. "In those days," Dies sighed, "my unhappy impression was that most Texas businessmen regarded me as an extremist, if not a crackpot."

## Gov. Edwin Edwards (D-Louisiana)

✪ Edwin Edwards served in Congress, and then became Louisiana's first Cajun governor. When asked about supposed illegal contributions to his campaign war chest, Edwards quipped, "It was illegal for them to give, but not for me to receive."

✪ In 1983 Edwards ran for governor of Louisiana against Republican David Treen. Edwin, who was the subject of eleven grand-jury investigations, described Treen as "so slow it takes him an hour and a half to watch *60 Minutes.*" Edwards declared that he couldn't lose unless he was caught "in bed with a dead girl or a live boy." After Treen lost the race, the Republican sighed, "It's difficult for me to explain Edwards's popularity. But how do you explain why nine hundred people drank spiked Kool-Aid with Jim Jones?"

✪ Even though Edwin won the gubernatorial election, he was indicted for allegedly taking payments from hospitals, which reputedly he used to pay off $2 million in gambling debts at Nevada casinos. To hide his losses, Edwards supposedly gambled under the aliases, "T. Wong," "T. Lee," "B. True," and "Ed Neff." Casino operators testified that the Louisiana politico paid with bags stuffed with cash, but he was acquitted.

✪ After Edwards left his wife of forty years and began socializing with a twenty-six-year-old nursing student, he quipped, "A man is as old as the woman he feels."

## Rep. Geraldine Ferraro (D-New York)

✪ In 1984 Ferraro ran for vice president, sharing the ticket with presidential candidate Walter Mondale. When business dealings of Ferraro's husband, John Zaccaro, came under scrutiny, Ferraro said that she had tried unsuccessfully to convince her husband to release his financial records. The New York congresswoman explained, "You people married Italian men, you know what it's like."

## Rep. Barney Frank (D-Massachusetts)

✪ In the spring of 1985, Frank reportedly answered a classified ad placed by a callboy in a Washington, D.C., gay publication. Stephen L. Gobie came to Frank's apartment and allegedly had sex with the congressman for $80. As they got to know each other better, Frank learned that Stephen was on probation for cocaine possession. Barney supposedly wrote letters to Gobie's probation officer on congressional stationery, asking that the young man be allowed to live in Washington and work for him. Stephen did housework and chauffeured Barney. At the same time, Stephen allegedly started operating an escort service from Frank's apartment. Stephen claimed that Barney knew about it, but Frank denied his statement and had Stephen leave the residence.

## REP. WAYNE HAYS (D-Ohio)

✪ From 1974 to 1976, Rep. Wayne Hays was purportedly involved with an attractive blonde named Elizabeth Ray who worked in his office. Ray claimed, "I can't type. I can't file. I can't even answer the phone." She claimed that when Wayne came to her apartment, "he walks right into the bedroom and looks at the digital clock. He's home by nine-thirty."

✪ In 1975, Hays divorced his wife and wed his secretary, who lived in Ohio. After the union, he told Elizabeth Ray to come to the office more often. Ray supposedly asked, "Do I still have to screw you?" Ray later blabbed to the press about her affair. She said, "I don't hate him, I'm a nervous wreck. I'm afraid of him." A fellow congressman once called Hays "the meanest man in Congress."

## JOHN JOHNSON (ex-member, Campisi crime family)

✪ Wearing an American flag around his neck, John Johnson announced his candidacy for the mayor of Austin, Texas. He then revealed that his real name was John Patrick Tully, and described himself as "a Mafia hoodlum, a gangster, and, in one case, a trigger man," who was reportedly once a member of the New Jersey–based Campisi crime family. Johnson/Tully explained that he had moved to Austin in 1982 under the witness-protection program, and had operated a hot dog vending business for nine years under an assumed identity. So why did he want to run for mayor? "I joined this mayoral race because I was in fear for my life from the Austin Police Department," he explained. "If they're gonna hit me, they're gonna hit me out in the limelight."

## DENNIS KUCINICH (D-Ohio)

✪ Kucinich was elected mayor of Cleveland in 1977. In April 1978, one of his appointees ordered three people to conduct an after-hours search of a Republican city official's office. The three burglars discovered two unopened bottles of liquor, drank them, got drunk, and began searching. When a safe dropped on one burglar's foot, he swung out his arm in pain and smacked another of his squad, and the third burglar then slugged him. The intruders left the office a mess, having discovered no improper documents.

✪ When city council members ordered an investigation of the alleged burglary, Kucinich called them "buffoons, lunatics, and fakers." The council refused to act on any of Dennis's initiatives and declared a recall vote. Kucinich won by 236 votes out of 120,000 cast.

✪ Cleveland was in desperate financial shape and the city's books apparently were so poorly maintained that they were declared "unauditable." Meanwhile, Dennis accused banks of "systematically looting Cleveland's financial resources," and forced the metropolis to default on its bonds. His detractors called Dennis a "lunatic." "Lunatic" Dennis lost his bid for reelection as mayor, but was elected to the U.S. House of Representatives from Ohio's 10th District in 1996.

## STATE REP. GIB LEWIS (D-Texas)

✪ Democratic Speaker of the Texas House of Representatives Gib Lewis addressed a group of people in wheelchairs on Disability Day, and asked, "Will y'all stand and be recognized?"

## REP. MICHAEL "OZZIE" MYERS (D-Pennsylvania)

✪ Representative Myers was caught on videotape in the Abscam sting operation (the same FBI mission that trapped Rep. John Jenrette). Myers was shown on tape taking money from a phony sheikh and boasting, "Bull**** walks, money talks."

## REP. WILBUR MILLS (D-Arkansas)

✪ Sixty-five-year-old Rep. Wilbur Mills lost interest in politics after a failed 1972 presidential campaign. Instead, he became intrigued with Anabella Battistella, better known as stripper Fanne Foxe, the Argentine Firecracker. Reportedly, the longtime chairman of the House Ways and Means Committee spent $1,700 a night buying champagne for his girlfriend, and in October 1974 took his show on the road. At 2:00 A.M. Washington, D.C., police stopped his blue Lincoln Continental for speeding and not having his headlights turned on. The car pulled over near the Tidal Basin, a ten-foot-deep estuary of the Potomac River. A tall, hysterical, blonde woman (Fanne Foxe) with two black eyes ran from the stopped vehicle and jumped into the water. As one policeman fished out the blonde, another law enforcer confronted a seemingly drunken Mills, who shouted, "I'm a congressman and I'll have you demoted."

⭐ Shortly after the incident, which was covered by a local TV station, Mills ran for reelection with the campaign slogan, "Don't go out with foreigners who drink champagne." He won.

⭐ In the long run, Foxe's attractions proved too strong for Wilbur. In December 1974, he flew from Washington to Boston to catch her act. "Mr. Mills, Mr. Mills, where are you?" asked Foxe from the stage. Mills appeared onstage, took a bow, and left. "This won't ruin me," Wilbur told reporters when photos of his escapade appeared nationally. "Nothing can ruin me." Wrong. His political career was over.

## SEN. CAROL MOSELEY-BRAUN (D-Illinois)

⭐ In 1992 Moseley-Braun became the first African-American woman elected to the U.S. Senate. After winning the election, she took a month's vacation to Africa with her campaign manager and fiancé Kgosie Matthews. In 1996, Senator Moseley-Braun returned to Nigeria with Matthews, who had become a registered agent of the Nigerian government. The senator had a secret meeting with the Nigerian dictator General Sani Abacha. When she was rebuked by government officials for lending legitimacy to the brutal despot, Moseley-Braun defended herself by saying, "It was like going to the hardware store with no makeup on," and added, "Do you call a press conference when you go on vacation?"

## SHORTY PRICE (D-Alabama)

⭐ Shorty Price called himself "the clown prince" of Alabama politics, and ran for governor in 1958. The five-foot-three-inch-tall candidate sought voter support by chewing cigars, and by getting gloriously drunk at the Alabama-Auburn football game, where he was arrested for allegedly peeing on a fire hydrant. Shorty complained about his arrest, saying that he didn't "have as many rights as a damn common dog." Nonetheless, he lost the gubernatorial race.

## CATHOMAS STARBIRD (D-California)

⭐ In 1998, Cathomas Starbird launched an anti-violence campaign and won election to the school board in Sausalito, California. Later it was revealed that six weeks before the election, Starbird had gone out to celebrate her husband's birthday with her spouse and a female friend. After drinks and dinner, the trio returned to Starbird's houseboat and reportedly began to remove their clothes. When her female pal refused to perform a sex act on her husband, Starbird allegedly punched her, jumped on her, and bit her face. Starbird pled guilty to assault, then refused to resign from the school board.

⭐ Later, it was revealed that Starbird had stabbed her husband with a kitchen knife during a fight three years before the biting incident. When a group of parents demanded that African-American Starbird resign her school-board post, her supporters declared them racist. "Historically, African-Americans are forgiving people," one supporter said. "Obviously, people of European descent aren't as quick to forgive and move on."

## GOV. GENE TALMADGE (D-Georgia)

⭐ Sporting red suspenders, rumpled suits, and messy hair, Gene Talmadge liked to portray himself as a country boy and called himself "the wild man from Sugar Creek." On the way to a barbecue and rally to open his 1942 gubernatorial campaign, one of Talmadge's associates recalled that the politician "had to take a crap." Trying to maintain his good-ole-boy image, the associate said, Talmadge "liked to go to the middle of the woods to let nature run his course." But this time, Talmadge got into trouble. According to the associate, "He got out there with that tallywhacker of his switching around in the wiregrass, and a black widow spider bit him right on the end of it. He said it liked to have killed him." Gene's appendage was so sore, he had to quit in the middle of his speech and let his buddy "Hellbent" Edwards take over for him. After he lost the election, Talmadge claimed he would have won "if that black widow hadn't bitten me on the balls."

## REP. JAMES A. TRAFICANT (D-Ohio)

⭐ James A. Traficant enjoyed writing poetry that he would recite on the House floor in the 1990s. Two samples: "When you hold this economy to your nosey, this economy is not rosy," and, "I say it is time for the American consumers to tell Nike to take a hikey."

⭐ When Traficant read in 1998 that only 7 percent of scientists believe in God, he made the following remarks on the floor of the House: "Most of these absentminded professors cannot find the toilet. Mr. Speaker, I have one question for these wiseguys to constipate over: How can something come from nothing? And while they digest that, Mr. Speaker, let us tell it like it is. Put these super-cerebral master debaters in some foxholes with bombs bursting all around them, and I guarantee they will not be praying to Frankenstein. Beam me up."

# REP. CHARLES WILSON (D-Texas)

⭐ Congressman Wilson allegedly bounced eighty-one checks from the House of Representatives bank, including a $6,500 payment made out to the Internal Revenue Service. However, when he was criticized for his financial sloppiness, Wilson got defensive. "It's not like molesting young girls or young boys," he snorted. "It's not a showstopper."

⭐ In the late 1970s, Wilson traveled to Nicaragua and gained a reputation as Congress' foremost defender of Nicaraguan dictator Anastasio Somoza. "I just generally got tired of these assaults on right-wing dictatorships," Charlie explained. " So I just said, 'No more.' " Wilson explained that Somoza's repression had to be put into perspective. "It's all relative. West Texas jailhouses on Saturday night are pretty rough."

⭐ Wilson took credit for driving the Russians out of Afghanistan, and asserted, in 1992, "I don't think there's any member of Congress who can lay claim to as large a contribution as I have made to defeating the Red Army."

⭐ Charlie liked to disguise himself in Afghan garb and sneak into the war zone on the border of Pakistan and Afghanistan. He purportedly often took girlfriends with him to rebel bases in Pakistan. On one such junket, Wilson brought along Miss World U.S.A. Annelise Ilshenko. When the U.S. Defense Intelligence Agency protested and refused to fly Wilson and Miss World U.S.A. to the rebel base, Charlie had the planes transferred to the National Guard.

# Huey Long

## FACTS OF LIFE (and Death)

ORiGiN: Born Huey Pierce Long Jr., August 30, 1893, Winnfield, Louisiana; died September 10, 1935, of bullet wounds received thirty-six hours earlier, in an assassination attempt.

FORMATIVE YEARS: Attended University of Oklahoma, 1912; attended Tulane University, 1914—never received a law degree but passed the Louisiana State Bar in 1915.

FAMILY PLANNING: Married Rose McConnell (stenographer), April 12, 1913.

SELECTED ELECTION SCORECARD: 1924: lost, governor, Louisiana. 1928: won, governor, Louisiana. 1930: won, U.S. Senate, Louisiana. (Assassinated in 1935.)

## QUICKIE BIO

In the spicy gumbo that is Louisiana political history, Huey Long was definitely the biggest cracker. Born in a log house, Huey detested farm work and made his brother do his fighting for him. Huey refined his political skills as a gambler and a salesman who pitched everything from starch to patent medicines. Brilliant and nervous, an insomniac and a voracious reader with a near perfect memory, he practiced law for ten years before getting into politics. After being elected governor of Louisiana, Long handed out free textbooks, built charity hospitals, paved roads, and created a state political machine so efficient he could operate it while serving as a U.S. senator in Washington, D.C. Shouting, "Share the wealth," and, "Every man a king," Huey gave himself the nickname "Kingfish" from a character on the radio show *Amos 'n' Andy*. "Politicians are the riffraff of a party," Long observed. "I'm different. I'm a Kingfish."

## HUEY LONG DOES
## THE DUMBEST THINGS

⭐ In 1927, Long encountered a political opponent in the lobby of a fancy New Orleans hotel. When the rival called Huey a liar, Long hit him a glancing blow to the jaw, then ran to the elevator. The other man chased after Huey and jumped onto the elevator. Huey emerged from the elevator with his opponent's cuff links and declared himself the winner of the fight. The "loser" claimed that Huey had huddled in the elevator "like a terror-stricken kitten." One eyewitness of the battle royal said that she couldn't see much of Huey because his head was lost in his opponent's stomach.

⭐ "In some ways he didn't act like a normal human being," observed one of Huey's companions. "He would reach over and take your meal and eat it."

⭐ Pointing to one of his supporters and political appointees, Governor Long bragged, "He's the best employee in the whole state. He does his work better than anybody we got." When asked, "What does he do, Huey?" the Kingfish replied, "Not a goddamn thing."

⭐ When a German ship docked in New Orleans, the captain visited Governor Huey in his hotel suite. The foreigner was wearing a full dress uniform. The Kingfish was sporting green pajamas, a red-and-blue lounging robe, and blue bedroom slippers. One reporter described Huey as looking like "an explosion in a paint factory."

⭐ The Kingfish became a football fan and attended many games in his home state. During one gridiron bash, a LSU (Louisiana State University) player complained that he had a boil on his leg. Huey cooked up a cure with Epsom salts and made the young man drink it. The player began to vomit in the second half of the game, but kept playing. He puked so bad that his team members wouldn't let him in the huddle, or stand near them on the line of scrimmage. Some thought it was a strategy devised by Huey, "the lonesome end."

⭐ Long was an avid golfer. In New Orleans he scored 115, but in Baton Rouge he always scored much lower. The reason was that in Baton Rouge

"Hell, I had a band of twelve pieces in my campaign that made more noise than yours does," shouted Huey Long (seated) to the members of the Louisiana State University marching band. When he wasn't playing the Jew's harp, Governor Huey enjoyed leading the LSU band at football games, waving a baton.
(Courtesy of Archive Photos)

he hired two black guys, "Coal Oil" and "Cornfield," to retrieve his badly hit balls and put them in good spots on the course.

⭐ Just before the U.S. Senate election of 1930, a man named Sam Irby said that he could prove that Gov. Huey Long's administration was corrupt. Earl, Huey's brother, suggested, "Let's take the son of a bitch and kill him." Huey kicked Earl in the butt. Instead, Governor Huey had Irby arrested and taken to a remote camp in south Louisiana.

⭐ While Huey served in the Senate, his handpicked yes-man, O.K. Allen, labored as governor of Louisiana. O.K. was not much of a politician. At a rally, he spotted a boy he thought he recognized and asked, "How's your father?" "Dead," the boy answered. Allen moved on through the crowd and then met the youngster again. "How's your father?" the governor asked. The boy answered, "Still dead."

⭐ After Huey died, his younger brother Earl became governor of Louisiana. Once, while talking with reporters in the lobby of the Roosevelt Hotel in New Orleans, Earl turned his back and peed on the floor.

⭐ Uncle Earl, as he was nicknamed, loved to buy things. During one supermarket shopping spree, he purchased one hundred pounds of potatoes, $300 worth of alarm clocks, eighty-seven dozen goldfish, and two cases of Mogen David wine.

★ In the late 1950s, Gov. Earl Long started dating the stripper Blaze Starr and partying with other women. In the evenings, the state police would escort the governor from his mansion in Baton Rouge to the red-light district of New Orleans. While the state's chief executive entertained women in a private room, the state police stood by the door. At one time, a state policeman heard a female scream inside the governor's room, and knocked on the door. A furious Governor Long shouted out, "You stupid a**! I told you to come to get me if I screamed, not if she screamed."

★ Earl partied so much it literally drove him crazy. In May 1959, he stood up in front of the Louisiana State Legislature and delivered an incoherent and irrational diatribe for ninety minutes. After state troopers escorted him back to the governor's mansion, Earl ripped his bed apart, threw a bottle of milk of magnesia through a window, and shouted, "Murder!"

★ Earl's wife had him committed. The governor was flown to a psychiatric clinic in Galveston. He spent two weeks in Texas, then filed a habeas corpus lawsuit against his spouse and returned to Louisiana, where his wife had him committed again.

★ In the hospital, Earl complained that he was "stuck with hypodermics and harpoons," and filed separation papers from his spouse, which prevented her from recommitting him. Then Governor Long fired the state-appointed superintendent of the hospital and hired a friend who ordered his immediate release.

★ After being freed from the institution, Governor Long went out West where he bet thousands of dollars on horse races and covered his head with a pillow case to avoid press photographers.

★ When he returned to Louisiana, Earl Long ran for the U.S. House of Representatives wearing a button that said, "I'm Not Crazy." The sixty-five-year-old politician won the election, but died ten days later, on September 5, 1960.

# Adam Clayton Powell Jr.

## FACTS OF LIFE (and Death)

**ORIGIN:** Born Adam Clayton Powell Jr., November 29, 1908, New Haven, Connecticut; died April 4, 1972, Miami, Florida, of cancer.

**FORMATIVE YEARS:** Colgate University, B.A., 1930; Columbia University, M.A. in religious education, 1932.

**FAMILY PLANNING:** Married Isabel Washington (actress), March 8, 1933; divorced, 1944; married Hazel Scott (singer), August 1, 1945; divorced, 1960; married Yvette Flores (Puerto Rican socialite), December 1960.

**SELECTED ELECTION SCORECARD:** 1944–66: won, U.S. House of Representatives, 10th District, New York (removed from office by fellow members of the House). 1967: won, U.S. House of Representatives, 10th District, New York (in a special election called by the U.S. Supreme Court). 1968: won, U.S. House of Representatives, 10th District, New York. 1970: lost, U.S. House of Representatives, 10th District, New York.

## QUICKIE BIO

In 1937, Powell inherited the pastorship of his father's Abyssinian Baptist Church in Harlem and kept it for the next thirty-four years. Adam used his pulpit for politics, and was elected to the New York City Council before winning a seat in Congress in 1945. The halls of Congress were still quite segregated when Powell first arrived in Washington, D.C. The New York preacher was the first African-American man to use the congressional shower room, the first to have a haircut in the congressional barbershop, and the first black man since 1908 to eat in the House dining room. "Mr. Speaker," the congressman told House Speaker Sam Rayburn, "I've got a bomb in each hand, and I'm going to throw them right away!" When he wasn't throwing "bombs," Adam was living the fast life. According to Andrew Young, the African-American leader who served as mayor of Atlanta, Georgia, "Rosa Parks integrated buses, James Meredith integrated the University of Mississippi, Martin Luther King Jr. integrated churches and lunch counters. But it was left to Adam Clayton Powell to integrate corruption."

## ADAM CLAYTON POWELL JR. DOES THE DUMBEST THINGS

✪ Described as a "man of great appetites," young pastor Powell enjoyed "beard" parties in Greenwich Village, in which strangers disguised their identities, had dinner, and matched up for sex.

✪ Adam's second wife, singer Hazel Scott, could keep up with him. She wore a low-cut dress to one party and wound up in the bedroom with a woman licking her back. "Honey," Hazel cooed, "if you're doing that for yourself, fine; if it's for me, a little lower and faster, please."

✪ Reverend Powell set up a tax assistance service at his Harlem church for the good of his parishioners. The three people who ran the service were indicted for income tax evasion, and two were convicted.

✪ In 1963, Powell traveled to Bimini (in the Bahamas) for the first time. He returned to the island many times and said he enjoyed it because it was "a place where I was 'Adam baby', or sometimes 'Mr. Jesus' to the people."

✪ "I'm not sure what this means," said Congressman Powell, when someone proposed a vaguely-worded amendment to one of his bills. "I suspect there may be a Caucasian in the woodpile."

✪ A fellow congressman visited Powell's office, ogled the beautiful secretaries, the Persian rugs, the fine Cuban cigars, and French wines. The guest said, "Mr. Chairman, you really go first-cabin." Adam smiled and replied, "Yes, these are the fruits of serving Jesus."

✪ In 1963, Powell accused Mrs. Esther James of being "a bag woman" for a numbers racket. James sued Powell for libel. Powell ignored the lawsuit for years. In 1967, a judge issued a warrant for his arrest. Powell fled to

Bimini for a year, and was only able to return to the United States to visit his district on Sundays, when legal papers could not be served. In Bimini, Adam told reporters that he would pay off the judgment in the suit with money from sales of his record, *Keep the Faith, Baby!*—a collection of his sermons. Esther James recorded a record of her own, entitled, *No Man is Above the Law—I Have Kept the Faith.*

★ While he was fighting the libel suit, Powell faced an investigation by fellow members of the House. Among other things, the scrutiny revealed that, apparently, Powell had put his estranged wife, who lived in Puerto Rico, on the payroll of his committee at $20,000 per year, then supposedly endorsed her paychecks, and kept the money for himself.

★ The House voted in February 1967 to exclude Powell from the House of Representatives. At the time he was residing in Bimini to avoid arrest in Harlem, he won a special reelection for another term in Congress, but did not show up to be sworn in. "I know that you will vote for me until I die," he once told his constituents. "And even after I'm dead I think some of you will write in my name."

★ After his reelection, Powell was deprived of seniority and his wages were garnished to pay a $25,000 fine. He rarely showed up in the House, and explained, "Part-time work for part-time pay." He finally lost his seat in 1970.

"I'm the only man in America that doesn't give a damn," bragged Rep. Adam Clayton Powell Jr., who didn't vote on the 1964 Civil Rights Act because he was reportedly too busy fishing on the island of Bimini.
(Courtesy of Archive Photos)

# Bonus Chapter
## Racist (and Race-Taunting) Democrats

**DUMBEST QUOTES**

"A strange and stupid race, the Anglo-Saxon."
(Boston Mayor James Michael Curley [D-Massachusetts])

"That's part of American greatness . . . discrimination. Yes, sir. Inequality, I think, breeds freedom and gives man opportunity."
(Gov. Lester Maddox [D-Georgia])

"Why would we have different races if God meant us to be alike and associate with each other?"
(Gov. Lester Maddox [D-Georgia])

"It's impossible for white folks to perceive reality."
(Rev. Jesse Jackson)

"Let us treat the Negro fairly. Give him justice; teach him that the white man is his real friend; let him know and understand once and for all that he belongs to an inferior race and that social and political equality will never be tolerated in the South."
(Sen. Theodore "The Man" Bilbo [D-Mississippi])

"White folks was in caves while we was building empires. . . . We taught philosophy and astrology and mathematics before Socrates and them Greek homos ever got around to it."
(Rev. Al Sharpton)

## QUICKIE PROFILE

It's dumb to make racist remarks, but such comments have long been used as a popular and powerful campaign tool for Democratic politicians. From the pro–slavery Democrats of the post-Civil War South and the pro-lynching Democrats of the 1890s, to the ethnic city bosses of the 1920s and the die-hard segregationists of the 1950s, Democrats have time and again run on racial issues and won. Some claim that members of minority groups cannot be considered racists because they do not have the power to oppress others. Okay. Maybe when minorities use outlandish racial taunts to win elections they are not being racist. But they are still being dumb. Black, white, or brown, time and again Democratic politicians have shown that when the going gets tough, the tough often start making dumb racial slurs.

## RACIST (AND RACE-TAUNTING) DEMOCRATS DO THE DUMBEST THINGS

✪ In Mississippi, Gov. James K. "The Great White Chief" Vardaman [D-South Carolina] always dressed in immaculate white outfits and rode to rallies in a lumber wagon pulled by white oxen. When Pres. Theodore Roosevelt invited black scientist Booker T. Washington to the White House for dinner in 1901, Vardaman referred to Roosevelt as a "coon-flavored miscegenationist," and said that he wouldn't be surprised "if the walls of the ancient edifice should become so saturated with the effluvia from the rancid carcasses that a chinch bug would have to crawl upon the dome to avoid asphyxiation."

✪ The "Great White Chief" Vardaman was a strong advocate of lynching "the Negro fiend." He told folks from the stump that he "would lead the mob to string the brute up, and I haven't much respect for the white man who wouldn't." Vardaman said educating blacks was a waste of money because an African-American was "a lazy, lying, lustful animal which no conceivable amount of training can transform into a tolerable citizen." Also, education would ruin a good field hand.

✪ The dumbest political contest in terms of racial nuttiness was the 1932 race for governor of South Carolina. During the campaign, Gov. Cole Blease (D-South Carolina) declared, "You can take a Negro, a tub of the hottest water you can get him into, and use all the soap you can use . . . and in five minutes he will smell just as offensive as he did before you washed him." His opponent, Ellison D. "Cotton Ed" Smith, gave the most disgusting speech in the history of American politics, known as

"The Speech." In it Cotton Ed described in graphic detail the rape of a white woman by "a big burly black brute" complete with howls, grunts, and groans. Who won? Smith.

✪ In the 1930s, Sen. Theodore "The Man" Bilbo (D-Mississippi) proposed legislation to deport twelve million blacks back to Africa and said, "God created the whites. I know not who created the blacks. Surely the devil created the mongrels."

✪ In 1956, under the leadership of Gov. James "Big Jim" Folsom (D-Alabama), the Alabama state legislature seriously considered barring the sale of Black & White Scotch, because of the name and the fact that the label showed two Scottish terriers, one black, one white, playing together. In that same year, the Alabama Senate voted unanimously to ask the U.S. Congress for money to transport all blacks out of the state.

✪ Eugene "Bull" Connor was a delegate at the 1948 Democratic National Convention in Philadelphia. Connor dressed up in a feathered head-dress and did a rain dance down the aisles of the convention hall, yelling that the Democrats should stop worrying about the civil rights of Negroes and do something for the downtrodden American Indian.

✪ Connor later became the police commissioner of Birmingham, Alabama. In 1961, he and his men learned that civil-rights protesters known as Freedom Riders would be arriving at the local bus station. Connor and the police department made a deal with the Ku Klux Klan that the Klan would have fifteen minutes to "greet" the Freedom Riders. As the pro-testers got off the bus, they were beaten, kicked, and clubbed. "Bull" Connor told the press that the beatings had occurred because his police department was shorthanded, due to Mother's Day vacations.

✪ In 1963, one of Gov. George Wallace's (D-Alabama) most trusted advi-sors was John Peter Kohn. "Now, George Wallace is not a racist," Kohn bragged. "I am." Kohn considered John F. Kennedy "the most dangerous man in the history of our country," and danced in the streets to cele-brate Kennedy's assassination.

✪ Wallace's main speechwriter in the early 1960s was Asa Carter, a well-known member of the Ku Klux Klan. Carter not only wrote the "segre-gation now, segregation tomorrow, segregation forever" speech, but penned a presentation that Wallace delivered on a tour of Northeast college campuses. In the talk, Governor Wallace declared that mulattos could handle college because they had "inherited the mentality and personality of their white ancestor" but were "not representative in any true sense of their less capable African half-brother." Wallace claimed later, "I was never saying anything that reflected upon black people."

★ Discussing his experiences at trade talks in Geneva, Switzerland, Sen. Ernest Hollings (D-South Carolina) observed, "You'd find these potentates from down in Africa, you know, rather than eating each other, they'd just come up and get a good square meal in Geneva."

★ In 1970, Jimmy Carter ran for governor of Georgia and shared the ticket with former Gov. Lester Maddox. Maddox owned the Pickrick restaurant in Atlanta, and made a name for himself in 1964 when he brandished a pistol and an ax handle and bought a newspaper ad which proclaimed, "Just in case some of you Communists, Socialists and other Integrationists have any doubt—THE PICKRICK WILL NEVER BE INTEGRATED!" The next year, Maddox closed the eatery to avoid integration.

★ At an off-the-record breakfast with an African-American reporter during the 1984 presidential campaign, Rev. Jesse Jackson referred to Jews as "Hymies" and called New York City "Hymietown." Later, at a New Hampshire synagogue, Jesse explained that his comments were not made "in the spirit of meanness."

★ When Black Muslim leader Louis Farrakhan introduced Jackson in Chicago in 1984, he told "the Jewish people," "If you harm this brother, I warn you in the name of Allah, this will be the last one you do harm."

★ Farrakhan told the black reporter who broke the "Hymie" story, "One day soon we will punish you with death." He added that the journalist's wife would "go to hell . . . the same punishment that's due that no-good, filthy traitor." Louis claimed later that he had not meant to threaten the man. At first, Jackson refused to speak against Farrakhan's remark, declaring, "My approach is to separate the sinner from the sin." Thereafter, Jackson declared that Farrakhan's remarks were "reprehensible and morally indefensible."

★ Ed Koch, mayor of New York City in the 1980s, referred to black Rep. Ron Dellums (D-California) as a "Watusi" and a "Zulu warrior." Ed claimed later that he meant the terms as a compliment. "My experience with blacks is that they're basically anti-Semitic," Koch once observed. "Now, I want to be fair about it. I think whites are basically anti-black."

★ Rep. Gus Savage (D-Illinois) once declared that Louis Farrakhan's claim that "Hitler was a great man" was "historically, culturally, and politically accurate."

✪ Savage was investigated by the House Ethics Committee for attacking a female Peace Corps volunteer in Africa. When asked by reporters to comment about the incident, Savage exploded, "I don't talk to you white motherf***ers . . . you bitch motherf***ers in the white press. . . . F*** you, you motherf***ing a**holes." Savage called the investigation a white racist attack and won reelection in 1990.

✪ After Mel Reynolds [D-Illinois] won the election to the U.S. House of Representatives, a magazine reported that Congressman Reynolds used to show up at college exams with his arm in a sling. When the magazine asked him if he had used this technique to get out of taking exams, Reynolds replied, "People always talk about African-Americans because they are racist pigs." The same publication reported that whenever Reynolds had failed an exam, he had claimed that his professors were racist.

✪ At rallies in the 1990s, the Rev. Al Sharpton derided whites as "faggots," and described blacks who didn't agree with him as "cocktail-sip Negroes" who carried "that German cracker's books under their arms." That German cracker was Karl Marx.

✪ During the 2000 presidential race, Al Gore's campaign manager, Donna Brazile, offered the following observation concerning black Republicans. "Republicans bring out Colin Powell and J. C. Watts because they have no program, no policy. They play that game because they have no other game. They have no love and no joy. They'd rather take pictures with black children than feed them." Ouch! Watts (R-Oklahoma) accused Brazile of "racist remarks" while Powell complained that Gore was letting Brazile play the "race card."

# Mel Reynolds

## FACTS OF LIFE

**ORIGIN:** Born Mel Reynolds, January 8, 1952, Mound Bayou, Mississippi.

**FORMATIVE YEARS:** Chicago City College, A.A. 1972; University of Illinois, B.A., 1974; attended Yale University for one semester, 1972; attended but did not graduate from Yale Law School, Harvard Law School, and the Kennedy School of Government at Harvard University; also attended Oxford University in England as a Rhodes scholar.

**FAMILY PLANNING:** Married Marisol, 1985; divorced, 1997.

**SELECTED ELECTION SCORECARD:** 1988–90: lost, U.S. House of Representatives, 2nd District, Illinois. 1992–94: won, U.S. House of Representatives, 2nd District, Illinois.

## QUICKIE BIO

Rarely in the course of human history does a politician as seemingly bizarre as Mel Reynolds rear his unwelcome head (unless you consider his immediate predecessor in office, Gus Savage). Born to a poor family in Mississippi and raised on the West Side of Chicago, Reynolds went to all the best schools, though he never graduated from most of them, and became the darling of the Chicago Democratic establishment. In his freshman term in Congress, Mel was even appointed to the powerful House Ways and Means Committee. But, oh, how quickly Reynolds's star faded. After a teenage campaign worker who became his girlfriend turned against him, Reynolds was the focus of one of the most sensational trials in Chicago political history. Police recordings of Reynolds and the teenager were supposedly so nasty

117

that they were edited before they were played for the jury. The whole Mel Reynolds thing was so incredibly dumb that even the *National Enquirer* refused to cover the case. "It's too sordid for us," the tabloid's news editor explained. "We're a family publication."

## MEL REYNOLDS DOES THE DUMBEST THINGS

✪ Reynolds ran against Rep. Gus Savage (D-Illinois) in 1988. In that same year, Savage went on an official visit to Zaire in Central Africa. The Illinois congressman met a female Peace Corps worker who was sent to brief him. Reportedly he grabbed her, kissed her, and tried to force her to have sex. When a reporter asked him about the incident, Savage snarled, "Get the f*** out of my face."

✪ During the 1992 campaign against Gus Savage for the House seat, Mel claimed he had been the victim of a drive-by shooting and accused Gus of inciting the incident. During his press conference, Mel wore a large Band-Aid on his forehead and didn't take it off for the remainder of the campaign. Savage claimed the episode was a hoax. No bullet was ever found, and the police closed their investigation of the incident without making any arrest. Some people thought it was strange that the window of the car in which Reynolds was sitting when he claimed he was shot was completely shattered, yet he had only suffered a Band-Aid-sized scratch.

✪ Between 1988 and 1993, Mel was sued sixteen times for allegedly writing bad checks on his personal and campaign bank accounts.

✪ Mel fired a congressional aide after the individual told reporters that Reynolds beat his wife. Reynolds's spouse issued a denial of the charges. But eighteen months later, she changed her story. She then claimed that her husband had beat her with his fists mostly, but "there were instances where he used objects, chairs, his feet, his shoes . . ."

✪ Congressman Reynolds's teenage girlfriend, Beverly Heard, who had worked on his campaign, went to the police and accused him of sexual assault. Then she retracted her accusations. Why? Heard's attorney, who was later arrested for possession of cocaine, was accused of supposedly accepting payment from the politician for shutting up his client.

✪ Reynolds was arrested and charged with sexual assault and obstruction of justice. A charge of child pornography was tacked on after police recorded Reynolds asking Heard to buy a Polaroid camera so that they could take nude pictures of a fictitious fifteen-year-old girl that Heard had invented to entrap Mel. "You may not want to tell her that, that age thing . . ." Reynolds told Heard on tape. "That would screw me."

★ Not only was Reynolds convicted of child pornography, sexual assault, and obstruction of justice, but, in a second trial a year later, he also was found guilty of lying to defraud banks, and of diverting campaign money into his personal accounts. During the second trial, Reynolds silently mouthed the words "you son of a bitch" at one of the witnesses, and was threatened with further prosecution.

★ After going to prison, Reynolds embarked on a hunger strike. Mel claimed that he had relented only when prison guards force-fed him french fries.

# Ann Richards

## FACTS OF LIFE

**ORIGIN:** Born Dorothy Ann Willis, September 1, 1933, Lakeview, Texas. (Later, she dropped the name Dorothy because it sounded too "country.")

**FORMATIVE YEARS:** Baylor University, B.A., 1954; University of Texas at Austin, teaching certificate, 1955.

**FAMILY PLANNING:** Married David Richards (lawyer), May 1953; divorced, 1984.

**SELECTED ELECTION SCORECARD:** 1990: won, governor, Texas. 1994: lost, governor, Texas.

## QUICKIE BIO

Ann Richards was the large-coifed hope of the Democratic Party, a sharp-tongued granny who blazed into the Texas governor's office, and blazed out after only one term. Born and raised in small-town Texas, Ann was a wild one who smoked hand-rolled cigars and once imitated Superman by jumping off the roof of her home. After she married a politically-active liberal lawyer and moved to Austin, Texas, Richards raised four kids, organic vegetables, and chickens that gave blue eggs. She taught junior high school, and led an energetic social life, partying her way into the inner circle of Texas state politics as she worked on state campaigns and won local elections. Ann served for eight years as Texas State Treasurer, joined Alcoholics Anonymous, and became the first woman governor of Texas since Miriam "Ma" Ferguson, who won in 1925 and was the first female ever elected governor of any state. Ma knew how to speak her own mind, especially against bilingual education: "If the English language was good enough for Jesus Christ," Ma claimed, "it's good enough for the schoolchildren of Texas." Who was the savvier politician, Ma or Ann? Ma won the governorship twice; Ann won only once.

## ANN RICHARDS DOES
## THE DUMBEST THINGS

⭐ Ann sent out a Christmas card one year with two women dressed as Mary and Joseph in the stable and the caption, "It's a girl."

⭐ Richards became a famous Austin, Texas, hostess and appeared at parties dressed as Santa Claus or Dolly Parton. At later public gatherings, Richards appeared as a male chauvinist pig, Harry Porco, complete with a pig snout. When she ran for statewide office, her supporters shuddered: "What if someone got tapes of Ann as Harry Porco?"

⭐ When asked about Ann's drinking, friends said she had a problem, but they couldn't recall anything she had done because they were drinking so much themselves.

⭐ In 1976, Ann won election as county commissioner. She went out at one point to talk to the members of a county road crew. When she questioned the workers, no one answered until she saw a dog and asked, "What's the dog's name?" The crew answered "Ann Richards." Later they changed the canine's name to "Miz Richards."

⭐ Ann first rose to national political prominence when she gave the keynote address at the 1988 Democratic National Convention, and spoke the following words: "For eight straight years, George Bush hasn't displayed the slightest interest in anything we care about. And now he's after a job he can't get appointed to, he's like Columbus discovering America—he's found child care, he's found education. Poor George, he can't help it—he was born with a silver foot in his mouth." Bush sent her a silver pin the shape of a foot, and won the presidential election.

⭐ Republican rancher and oilman Clayton "Claytie" Williams opposed Ann in the 1990 gubernatorial campaign. Claytie declared, "I'm not a politician, I'm a Bubba," and ran TV ads in which he offered to send drug users to jail and teach them "the joys of bustin' rocks." When asked what he'd do with all those busted rocks, Claytie said he'd turn them into picnic benches.

"I haven't seen a crowd like this since the last Commander Cody concert at the Armadillo," said Texas Governor Ann Richards, who liked to entertain friends with her imitation of Harry Porco, the male chauvinist pig.
(Courtesy of Texas State Library and Archives Commission)

✪ Rumors circulated that Claytie sponsored "honey hunts" on his ranch, during which the candidate and his friends supposedly chased prostitutes through the greasewood and mesquite. Claytie denied that he led honey hunts. But he did allow as to how he had patronized the red-light districts of Mexican border towns during his college days, explaining, "It was the only way you got serviced then."

✪ Williams invited reporters out to the ranch in west Texas. They were sitting around, when a drizzle started. Looking heavenward, Williams delivered some tumbleweed philosophy. He told the damp journalists that weather was "sort of like rape. If you know it's inevitable, just lay back and enjoy it."

✪ When Ann was accused of doing drugs, she explained that she had been so drunk in those years that she could not remember what she had done.

✪ To show how tough she was, candidate Richards invited photographers along for a dove hunt. She fired off her shotgun several times, at a completely empty sky.

✪ At a banquet in Austin, Claytie encountered Richards. When she offered him her hand, Claytie fumed, "I'm not gonna shake your hand. Ann Richards, I'm here today to call you a liar." Richards replied sweetly, "Oh, I'm sorry, Clayton," and won the election.

✪ Ann got almost as nasty as Clayton Williams during her 1994 gubernatorial campaign against Republican George W. Bush. She called her opponent "Shrub" and "Junior" and described him as "the young Bush boy" who was "missing his Herbert."

✪ As things went downhill in 1994, Governor Ann got frustrated with George W. and moaned, "You just work like a dog, do well, the test scores are up, the kids are looking better, the dropout rate is down, and all of a sudden you've got some jerk who's running for office telling everybody it's all a sham and it isn't real." Bush responded, "The last time I was called a jerk was at Sam Houston Elementary School in Midland, Texas." He won the election.

# Franklin Delano Roosevelt

## All-American Presidential Bonus Chapter

---

### DUMBEST QUOTES

"I have said this before, but I shall say it again and again and again: Your boys are not going to be sent into any foreign wars."

**(FDR in 1940, shortly before committing the U.S. to World War II)**

"I think that if I give [Russia's Joseph Stalin] everything I possibly can and ask for nothing from him in return . . . he won't try to annex anything and will work with me for a world of democracy and peace."

---

## FACTS OF LIFE (and Death)

**ORIGIN:** Born January 30, 1882, Hyde Park, New York; died April 12, 1945, Warm Springs, Georgia, of a stroke.

**FORMATIVE YEARS:** Harvard University, B.A., 1903; studied at Columbia University Law School but never graduated.

**FAMILY PLANNING:** Married Anna Eleanor Roosevelt (socialite), March 17, 1905.

**SELECTED ELECTION SCORECARD:** 1914: lost, U.S. Senate, New York. 1929: won, governor, New York. 1932–44: won, U.S. president (he died in office on April 12, 1945).

## QUICKIE BIO

Writer Walter Lippmann once described FDR as "a pleasant man who, without any important qualifications for the office, would very much like to be president." The aristocratic Franklin Delano Roosevelt (FDR) turned out to be one of the greatest presidents in American history as well as a devious philanderer. The only person ever elected to be U.S. president four times, Roosevelt was born to a very wealthy family in Hyde Park, New York. Young FDR was headed for a promising political career when he was struck by polio in 1921. For the remainder of his life, he used leg braces and a wheelchair, but managed to hide, or downplay, the handicap from most of the American people. Franklin served as Assistant Secretary of the Navy, then governor of New York, and finally, U.S. president. In his acceptance speech before the Democrat Party in 1932, he declared, "The only thing we have to fear is fear itself," and promised "a New Deal for the American people." The New Deal proved to be an alphabet soup of federal relief agencies—the TVA, the SEC, the FDIC, the CCC, the PWA, the WPA, the AAA—designed to put money into the pockets of the beleaguered American voter suffering from the Great Depression. While he offered Americans the New Deal, Roosevelt gave his socially well-connected, but very plain-looking wife Eleanor a raw deal in their private life.

## FDR DOES
## THE DUMBEST THINGS

⭐ FDR's mother forced him to wear dresses until he was five years old.

⭐ As a youngster, FDR visited the White House and met Pres. Grover Cleveland. The chief executive bent down towards his young visitor and said, "My little man, I am making a strange wish for you—it is that you may never be president of the United States . . . "

⭐ FDR met his future wife Eleanor at the Harvard-Yale football game and soon asked for her hand in marriage. FDR's imperious mother didn't approve, and took her son on a Caribbean cruise to divert his attention. But FDR flirted with the women on board the ship so much that his mother changed her mind, and allowed him to wed Eleanor.

⭐ Eleanor's maiden name was Eleanor Roosevelt. She was FDR's fifth cousin once removed. FDR was not only related to his wife, he was related by blood or marriage to eleven other U.S. presidents.

★ After he became president, FDR invited Sen. Huey Long (D-Louisiana) over for lunch with the Roosevelt clan. Long wore a loud suit, a pink necktie, and an orchid shirt. At one point, Ma Roosevelt asked loudly, "Who is that *awful* man sitting next to my son?" Huey said nothing then, but commented later, "By God, I feel sorry for him. He's got even more sons of bitches in his family than I've got in mine."

★ In 1921, while Roosevelt was Assistant Secretary of the Navy, he launched an investigation of a ring of suspected homosexuals at the Naval training station in Newport, Rhode Island. The sleuths gathered incriminating evidence. How did they do it? By getting it on with the presumed gay men.

★ In the summer of 1916, Eleanor went away for the summer, while FDR stayed in Washington, D.C., and started an affair with his wife's secretary, Lucy Page Mercer. When Eleanor wrote to FDR and voiced suspicions, he replied, "You were a goosy girl to think or even pretend to think I don't want you here all the summer . . . "

★ Two years later, when Roosevelt got sick, Eleanor unpacked his luggage and found love letters from Lucy to her husband. She offered FDR a divorce, but he cried, "Don't be a goose!" He didn't want a marital breakup because it would have ruined his political career and cost him his inheritance. They remained married, but, according to their son, "through the entire rest of their lives, they never did have a husband-and-wife relationship . . . "

★ FDR continued to carry on with Lucy. While he was Assistant Secretary of the Navy, she served in the Navy and worked nearby. The couple liked to cruise on the Potomac River together.

★ Lucy finally married someone else. And FDR then started a liaison with Marguerite "Missy" LeHand, a campaign worker at FDR's Washington, D.C., headquarters. Missy became his secretary, and lived at the New York governor's mansion. FDR's kids often caught a nightgown-clad Missy in their father's room in the governor's mansion.

★ One time, Missy was discovered sitting on FDR's lap in the Oval Office at the White House.

★ FDR enjoyed spending time on a houseboat in Florida with Missy, and without Eleanor. Missy and FDR hung out in their pajamas so much that one observer called it a "negligee existence."

★ Eleanor knew all about Missy, but didn't complain. She became bosom buddies with a cigar-smoking journalist named Lorena Hickok. Eleanor

President Roosevelt liked to play with his dog, Fala. But when the President made a trip to the Aleutian Islands in 1944 he left his beloved doggy behind and sent a destroyer to fetch him. When Republicans criticized the doggy patrol Roosevelt said, "I don't resent the attacks, and my family doesn't resent the attacks—but Fala does resent them! His Scotch soul was furious. He has not been the same dog since."
(Courtesy of Franklin D. Roosevelt Library)

called her "Hick." Hick was a well-known lesbian who had lived openly with a woman. Hick admitted that she "went off the deep end" over females, and she certainly did so over Eleanor. She gave Eleanor a sapphire ring, which Mrs. Roosevelt wore to her husband's inauguration in 1933. The night before, Hick and Eleanor had shared a room at the Mayflower Hotel in Washington, D.C.

★ Hick wrote Eleanor, "Most clearly I remember your eyes with a kind of teasing smile in them, and the feeling of that soft spot just northeast of the corner of your mouth against my lips." In another letter, Hick wrote to Eleanor, "I want to put my arms around you and kiss you at the corner of your mouth. And in a little more than a week now—I shall." "Oh! I want to put my arms around you," Eleanor corresponded to the five-foot-eight-inch tall, two-hundred-pound Hick: "I ache to hold you close . . ." Eleanor confessed. "I love you beyond words and long for you. . . . Dear one, I wish you were here."

★ The first lady spent long periods of time alone with Hick in the White House bathroom, and explained to the staff that it was "the only place they could find privacy for a press interview."

✪ The sleeping arrangements during FDR's first term at the White House were truly bizarre. Hick had her own room, but usually slept on the day bed in Eleanor's room. Missy LeHand had her own suite next to the president, but she was often seen in the president's chambers at night in her nightgown. She was discreet enough to leave the room before the president was served breakfast in bed.

✪ Finally FDR got fed up. He referred to Hick and Eleanor's other female pals as "she-males" and at one time yelled about Lorena, "I want that woman kept out of this house!" After that outburst, the White House maids made sure that FDR and Hick did not cross paths.

✪ After Hickok fell in love with a female tax-court judge, Eleanor spent the night with Joseph Lash at a hotel in Chicago. Oops! Lash was under investigation and the room was bugged by Army intelligence. A FBI report later stated that the tapes "indicated quite clearly that Mrs. Roosevelt and Lash engaged in sexual intercourse."

✪ Eleanor allegedly took up with her physical trainer Earl Miller. Then Miller had an affair with FDR's girlfriend Missy. It was rumored that the chief executive engineered the affair so that Eleanor would not take off with Earl.

✪ Reporter Dorothy Schiff claimed that she had had sex with Roosevelt. "In a rather sweet way, he was fairly bold," she detailed, "and everything about his body—except his legs—was strong."

✪ While shaking hands in a receiving line, FDR got bored. So as he shook hands with each admirer, he said, "I murdered my grandmother this morning." Most people smiled and ignored the comment, but one supporter blurted out, "She certainly had it coming."

✪ Roosevelt was the first president ever to tape-record himself in the Oval Office. He was also the first chief executive to be embarrassed by what was recorded. During the presidential campaign of 1940, Roosevelt claimed that New York City Mayor Jimmy Walker "was living openly with this gal all over New York City, including the house across from me." Roosevelt described Walker's gal as "an extremely attractive little tart." FDR was also caught on tape telling his aides to start a whispering campaign about his opponent, Republican Wendell Wilkie, and his mistress.

✪ The king and queen of England visited FDR's palatial home in Hyde Park, New York, in the summer of 1939. After everyone was seated, a table in the dining room collapsed and sent plates crashing to the floor. "This is an old family custom," Roosevelt explained. "Think nothing of it!"

★ Later that same evening, a waiter coming downstairs tripped and fell, dropping a full tray of drinks. The next day, Roosevelt served the king and queen hot dogs at a picnic. At one point, FDR was crawling backwards across the lawn and landed in the middle of a tray full of drinks and food. Roosevelt later said of the visit, "Really, it's as funny as a crutch."

★ In reference to Nicaraguan dictator Anastasio Somoza, FDR observed, "He may be a son of a bitch, but he's our son of a bitch."

★ Black leaders approached Roosevelt to request that negroes be allowed to serve along with whites in World War II. Roosevelt told the black leaders that blacks would be given combat roles in the war, then reversed himself and allowed the military's policy of segregation to go unchanged. When black leaders complained, the president suggested a solution. "Since we are training a certain number of musicians on board ship—the ship's band—there's no reason . . . why we shouldn't have a colored band on some of these ships, because they're darn good at it . . ."

★ While a guest at the White House, Winston Churchill climbed out of the bathtub one evening and walked around his room naked. Roosevelt knocked on the door. "Come in, come in," Churchill responded. The president entered the room and was confronted by the fat, naked British politician. Churchill threw his arms wide apart and announced, "The Prime Minister of Great Britain has nothing to conceal from the president of the United States!" FDR was Churchill's seventh cousin once removed.

★ For many years, FDR hosted a cocktail party for his birthday and dressed as a Roman emperor. The female guests were expected to appear as vestal virgins. The president encouraged partygoers to join him in a cocktail with the words, "How about another little sippy?"

★ After Missy LeHand suffered a cerebral hemorrhage and passed away in 1941, and Lucy Mercer's husband died of a stroke, Lucy and FDR resumed their affair. FDR's daughter Anna helped arrange meetings between Lucy and the president without the knowledge of Eleanor. In 1945, Lucy vacationed with the president in Warm Springs, Georgia. The president was cracking jokes and laughing with his girlfriend when he suffered a cerebral hemorrhage, fell forward, and died. Lucy was hustled out of town before grieving wife Eleanor was hustled in.

# Pat Schroeder

## FACTS OF LIFE

ORIGIN: Born Patricia Scott, July 30, 1940, Portland, Oregon.

FORMATIVE YEARS: University of Minnesota, B.A., 1961; Harvard Law School, J.D., 1964.

FAMILY PLANNING: Married James White Schroeder (lawyer), August 18, 1962.

SELECTED ELECTION SCORECARD: 1972–96: won, U.S. House of Representatives, 1st District, Colorado.

## QUICKIE BIO

When Pat Schroeder was first elected to the House of Representatives in 1972, a senior congressman told her, "Politics is about thousand-dollar bills, Chivas Regal, Lear jets and beautiful women. So what are you doing here?" Pat didn't have much experience with booze or thousand-dollar bills. However, she was pretty good-looking and knew her way around an airplane. A pilot who worked her way through college operating an air charter service, Pat flew through Harvard Law School and married a liberal Democrat from Colorado. Her husband, who had lost a statewide race, encouraged her to make a poorly financed "kamikaze run" for Congress. Pat ran in part against the seniority system—then won and kept her seat in Congress for twenty-four years. In 1992, as more women entered Congress, an old-time politico griped at Pat and said, "Look what you've done. The place looks like a shopping center." And what was the title of this liberated woman's political autobiography? *24 Years of Housework and the Place is Still a Mess* (1998).

## PAT SCHROEDER DOES THE DUMBEST THINGS

✪ In 1971, Pat worked for Planned Parenthood and handed out buttons on Valentine's Day that said, "Vasectomy Means Never Having to Say You're Sorry."

✪ Schroeder always signed her name with a smiley face.

✪ When asked how she could serve in Congress and raise two kids, Pat Schroeder said, "I have a brain and a uterus and I use them both."

✪ When Pat first arrived in Congress, females were not allowed on the outdoor porch of the House chamber. According to Schroeder, the reason why was that "the congressmen—liked to pull off their trousers and sunbathe on the chaise lounges."

✪ When Pat was first elected to the House, she was appointed, along with Rep. Ron Dellums (D-California), to the powerful Armed Services Committee over the objections of committee chairman Rep. F. Edward Hebert (D-Louisiana). Hebert was so angry at their appointments that he ordered only one chair, not two, to be added to the committee room. Pat, the only woman on the committee, and Dellums, the only black, were thus required to share the same seat—for two years. Pat recalled, "We sat 'cheek to cheek' on one chair, trying to retain some dignity."

✪ In 1973, Schroeder commented on the typical debate over weapons systems: "Is it bigger? Is it faster? Is it more maneuverable? Does it give closer, more comfortable shaves?"

✪ Pat once dressed up in a rented Easter Bunny suit and handed out Easter eggs to children along the Great Wall of China.

✪ In a speech during the Reagan administration, Schroeder started the audience murmuring when she said that as a liberal she "felt like the little Dutch boy with his finger in the dike." Pat had forgotten that she was speaking to the Gertrude Stein Democratic Club of Washington. Gertrude Stein was a prominent lesbian literary figure.

⭐ Pat's most memorable line was the one about Reagan's "Teflon-coated presidency." Schroeder claimed that she came up with the quip while cooking breakfast, but a former aide doubted that she came up with the phrase at all. "That story is clearly not credible because the woman's never cooked in her life and wouldn't know what a Teflon pan is."

⭐ Actor John Wayne once visited Pat's congressional office and presented her with a silver cigarette lighter inscribed with the words "F*** communism." Pat refused to accept the lighter. When her husband found out, however, he was furious at her.

⭐ Pat was co-chairperson of the 1984 Gary Hart presidential campaign. He asked her to repeat the same task in 1987. At first she declined, citing rumors of Gary's infidelity. He denied them and she took on the job. One weekend, Pat flew to California to speak on Hart's behalf to a gathering of newspaper editors. Later she learned that Hart had spent this same weekend partying on the good boat *Monkey Business* with model Donna Rice. Pat's reaction? "Do you mean I've been canceling my schedule, flying to these godforsaken places, eating smoked hamster or whatever that airplane food is, while he's on a pleasure boat in Florida?"

⭐ After Hart dropped out of the presidential race in 1987, Pat jumped in as a substitute. Right away she had problems. One Democratic Party state chairman said that he couldn't support Pat because it would mean having "a man for first lady." As for Gary Hart, he endorsed New York governor Mario Cuomo for the nomination.

⭐ Pat described her campaign as "an unbelievable nightmare," and decided to withdraw from the race before any of the presidential primaries. When she announced her decision to the media, she cried, and was ridiculed by opponents, reporters, and comedians. Schroeder was so angry that she ordered her staff to collect data on tearful world leaders. The staff referred to the data as the "sob sister" file.

⭐ Years later Pat sighed, "What began on June 5, 1987, as an exciting quest for the presidency of the United States ended three months later ... as a search for Kleenex." She claimed, "I was into crying before it was cool."

# Rev. Al Sharpton

## FACTS OF LIFE

ORIGIN: Born Alfred C. Sharpton Jr., October 3, 1954, Brooklyn, New York.

FORMATIVE YEARS: Brooklyn College School of Contemporary Studies—majored in contemporary politics but dropped out.

FAMILY PLANNING: Married "briefly" to Marsha Tinsley (singer); married Kathy Jordan (backup vocalist for James Brown), 1975.

SELECTED ELECTION SCORECARD: 1992: lost, U.S. Senate, New York. 1994: lost, U.S. Senate, New York.

## QUICKIE BIO

New York is perhaps the most racist city in the country," declared the Rev. Al Sharpton, who has also said of his hometown, "This is the center of the world." Little Al liked to wear his mom's wigs, sing gospel music, and preach to his sister's dolls. He first sermonized to a real congregation when he was only four years old. By the time he was ten, Sharpton was an ordained minister and a child prodigy who preached all over the country. When preacher (and, later, civil-rights leader) Jesse Jackson met young Al, he said, "All you got to do is choose your targets and kick a\*\*." Sharpton emulated Jackson's style, and made a national reputation by getting himself involved in

133

"cases" for "clients" who requested his help in leading unauthorized marches and grabbing media attention. Some called Sharpton a loudmouth, a walking sound bite, a con artist, a charlatan, and, like commie-baiting Sen. Joe McCarthy (R-Wisconsin), "a practitioner of the big lie." But probably nobody said it better than Jesse Jackson who, at one point, looked at Sharpton and declared, "Here come the boy wonder, ain't gonna be nothing but a Harlem fanatic."

## REV. AL SHARPTON DOES THE DUMBEST THINGS

★ Sharpton worked with soul singer James Brown in the early 1970s. Brown was a supporter of Sharpton's National Youth Movement campaign. In 1974 Al promoted a fund-raising concert with James Brown at Madison Square Garden. With his $3,000 promoter's fee, Sharpton rented four fancy hotel suites and invited his mother. "She thought I was crazy," he confessed. "But I stayed there until I spent all my money, every dime."

★ In 1981, Sharpton was scheduled to go with James Brown to meet Vice President George Bush at the White House to help celebrate Martin Luther King Jr.'s birthday. Before they left for Washington, Brown took Sharpton to his hairdresser and said, "I want you to do the reverend's hair like mine, because when we go to the White House there's going to be a lot of press, and when people see him I want them to see me, like he's my son."

★ Sharpton later cut a record with Brown, entitled "God Has Smiled on Me."

★ After James took Al to his hair stylist, Brown pleaded, "Reverend, I want you to make me one promise. I want you to wear your hair like that until I die." Sharpton said fine. When Brown served time in jail, he frequently called Sharpton and asked, "Rev, how's your hair?" Sharpton's answer? "Just like you."

★ One of the groups Al complained about for their lack of involvement in African-American causes was the Jackson Five family, until they agreed to hire Sharpton to work on one of their concert tours. Sharpton organized "the Pride Patrol" of poor kids to work security at every venue. Some accused him of extortion, but for Al it was show biz.

★ In November 1987 Tawana Brawley, a fifteen-year-old black girl, was found covered in racist graffiti and dog feces in a plastic garbage bag on the grounds of an apartment complex in Duchess County in New

York State. Some said it was a hoax, but Sharpton claimed that Brawley had been kidnapped and raped by white law enforcement officials. To win support for Tawana's case, Sharpton posed for photographers sitting under a hair dryer at a salon. Al thought the picture mocked white society, but Rev. Jesse Jackson was furious and asked Sharpton, "Do you want to be remembered for hot curlers?"

★ Early in 1989, Sharpton was indicted on sixty-seven counts, including forty-three alleged felonies. The judge addressed Sharpton's lawyer and said, "Counselor, for the purposes of this arraignment, how does your client plead?" Al jumped in: "I plead the attorney general insane."

★ As officers escorted Al from the courtroom in handcuffs, they pushed his head down to get him into the police car. Sharpton popped his head back up and shouted, "He's messing up my hair!" Sharpton pleaded guilty to the misdemeanor of failing to pay his New York State taxes, and the felony convictions were dropped.

★ In January 1991, Sharpton attended a demonstration protesting the August 1989 killing of a black teenager shopping for a used car by Jews in the Bensonhurst neighborhood of Brooklyn. During the demonstration, Sharpton was stabbed. Rev. Jesse Jackson visited Sharpton in the hospital. Jesse told Al that the only reason he survived the attack was because he had seven inches of fat around his middle, and the knife blade was only six inches long.

"I created Al Sharpton. I wore my hair like this. I dressed like this. I talked like this. I weighed this much. That was my persona." So declared Rev. Al Sharpton, who referred to his closest followers as his "nut group."
(Courtesy of Ozier Muhammad/New York Times, Co./Archive Photos)

⭐ When Sharpton ran for the U.S. Senate in 1992, he declared that he "had the right to throw my hair in the ring." He insisted that he was the first person in the nation to run against two people who had arrested him.

⭐ Sharpton was arrested more than twenty times and jailed five times for protests which included stopping traffic on the Brooklyn-Queens Expressway, and closing the Statue of Liberty. "I never get a permit to march because I don't think I should have to, I thinks it's a human right to march. And every time someone asks me for a permit I say, 'I got my permit on October 3, 1954, when they gave me my birth certificate. And I didn't apply for that one.' "

# Glenn H. Taylor

## FACTS OF LIFE (and Death)

**ORIGIN:** Born Glenn Hearst Taylor, April 12, 1904, Portland, Oregon; died April 18, 1984, Burlingame, California.

**FORMATIVE YEARS:** Left school after the eighth grade.

**FAMILY PLANNING:** Married, 1922; divorced, 1929; married Dora Marie Pike (usher), March 1931.

**SELECTED ELECTION SCORECARD:** 1938–40: lost, U.S. Senate, Idaho. 1944: won, U.S. Senate, Idaho. 1948: lost, U.S. vice president (as a member of the Progressive Party). 1950: lost, U.S. Senate, Idaho.

## QUICKIE BIO

Singing cowboy" Glenn H. Taylor attracted national attention as "the least effective member of the Senate" and "one of the greatest speakers of our time." Taylor was the twelfth of thirteen children born to a former Texas Ranger (who was also a preacher and an auctioneer), who homesteaded in Idaho. Young Glenn worked as a sheepherder, a movie-house manager, a sheet-metal worker and a traveling performer. When the Depression hit, he found it hard to make money as a singing cowboy, and thus started to become interested in politics. He went to a political rally in 1937, saw Idaho governor C. Ben Ross and said to himself, "This man is a politician? Ben Ross is an actor." Taylor threw his ten-gallon hat into the ring three times before he launched a campaign on horseback with cowboy regalia and an election fund of $75 in 1944 and won a seat in the U.S. Senate. He lost his Senate post after bolting the Democratic Party to run as vice president with Henry Wallace's Progressive Party in 1948. Bald like his dad, Taylor had a vision in a dream: make men's hairpieces out of plastic. He got into hair and out of politics for good. "I listened to Glenn Taylor every time I got a chance," wrote Idaho novelist Vardis Fisher, "not because he said anything, but because he said nothing superbly well."

## GLENN H. TAYLOR DOES THE DUMBEST THINGS

★ Fifteen-year-old Taylor worked as a "canary," the male singer at an Idaho brothel. Taylor fell in love with one of his co-stars, Rosie, who could bend over backwards, put her head between her legs, and suck a five-inch cucumber into her mouth until just the tip was showing.

★ Glenn shared a house with the talented woman. They talked about love. "I can't say I've never done it," young Taylor explained shyly. "I have done it with Rosie.... I didn't think it would hurt anything. All the other farm boys were doing it.... She wouldn't get pregnant or anything.... I was only ten years old." The woman asked, "How old was she?" "Oh," Taylor thought, "about six months old." The woman was shocked. "Six months?" "Yes," Glenn nodded, "but she was almost as big as her mother." The woman shook her head, "What in the world are you talking about?" Taylor looked at her innocently and said, "Rosie, Old Brownie's calf."

★ Taylor and his housemate started having sex together. But when Taylor asked for her hand in marriage, she said she wasn't worthy. "So you've been around. . . ." Taylor reassured his beloved. "What of it? Did you ever make love to a calf? Well, I did!"

★ When he ran for the U.S Senate in 1940, Taylor described his opponent as someone who moved around "like a constipated turtle." Taylor had no problem with constipation. He was so broke at the time that he lived off a diet of peaches and oatmeal cookies which, Taylor admitted, "gave us the trots, or to put it less euphemistically, the runs."

★ Glenn was just as broke when he ran again for the Senate in 1942. He came up with a new idea, the Saddle Bag Campaign. For two months, he rode horseback across the state, wearing a maroon cowboy shirt emblazoned with the words "Taylor—Senate."

"There was corn enough for everybody, and to spare." Glenn Taylor (left front) commented about his group, the Glendora players. The group featured Glen's wife, Dora (right front), on trombone and their boy, Arod (center front). Arod was Dora spelled backwards. Taylor liked the name because it was "romantic sounding," "individualistic," and "easily remembered." Bragged Taylor, "You don't run into Arods every day."
(Courtesy of Idaho State Historical Society)

⭐ After losing his third statewide political race, Taylor reflected on the reason for his defeats. He understood that he had determination, wit, honesty, and humor. Then he realized that the one thing he didn't have was hair. Whenever he took his cowboy hat off, Taylor said, the ladies recoiled "like I had been scalped by Sitting Bull."

⭐ Taylor had tried hairpieces but claimed, "I couldn't find anything I'd wear to a dog fight." So after announcing his candidacy for the U.S. Senate in 1944, he sent out a press release claiming he had the flu, and set to work. He took the aluminum bottom of a bread pan, flesh-colored panties, and switches of human hair. He pounded the pan to the shape of his bald spot and spent ten days meticulously sewing the hairs in place. He glued the hairy panties to the aluminum, placed it on his head, looked in the mirror, and was seriously disappointed. The hairline was too abrupt.

⭐ Depressed, Glenn took a bath. He looked down—"Eureka!" He took scissors and went to work, "very carefully of course. This was a delicate operation. The success of my hairpiece, as well as my unimpaired manhood, were both at stake." Taylor glued his pubic hairs along the front of the hairpiece and, *voilà*, his merkin looked real!

⭐ The pube-headed Taylor won his election to the U.S. Senate. In October 1947, the senator from Idaho left Washington, D.C., and started to ride horseback across the U.S. to gain support for his pacifist views. He quit in mid-November, claiming that he had "bit off more than he could chew."

⭐ After losing his Senate seat, Glenn realized that making hairpieces was more financially rewarding than serving in Congress. "Not only was I going to get rich, but people were going to love me," said the founder of Taylor's Toppers, Inc. "Put a Topper on a guy and, no matter what his religion, politics, or nationality, you have a friend."

# George Wallace

## FACTS OF LIFE (and Death)

**ORIGIN:** Born George Corley Wallace Jr., Clio, Alabama, August 25, 1919; died September 13, 1998, Montgomery, Alabama, of heart failure.

**FORMATIVE YEARS:** University of Alabama Law School, LL.B., 1942.

**FAMILY PLANNING:** Married Lurleen Burns (sales clerk), May 22, 1943; widowed, May 6, 1968; married Cornelia Snively (divorced housewife), January 4, 1971; divorced, 1978; married Lisa Taylor (singer), 1981; divorced, 1987.

**SELECTED ELECTION SCORECARD:** 1958: lost, governor, Alabama. 1962: won, governor, Alabama. 1966: won, "governor," Alabama (his wife Lurleen Wallace actually won the contest because Wallace was forbidden by law from succeeding himself as governor). 1968–76: lost, U.S. president (with the American Independent Party). 1974: won, governor, Alabama. 1982: won, governor, Alabama.

## QUICKIE BIO

According to George Wallace, "The difference between a national Democrat and an Alabama Democrat is like the difference between a communist and a non-communist." George Wallace was different, all right. The skinny, scrappy, teetotaling, high-school Golden Glove boxer from southeast Alabama got involved with politics when he was barely sixteen years old, working as a page in the Alabama Senate. He served as a B-29 crew member in World War II, but for the rest of his life, George Wallace only cared about one thing—running for political office. He was so broke when he was elected to the Alabama House of Representatives that he had to hitchhike to the state capital, Montgomery. After he was defeated for governor in 1958, Wallace vowed, "I ain't never gonna be outnigguhed again." He wasn't. Instead, he became the poster boy for the redneck, racist element in the electorate of the South during the hard-fought civil-rights struggle of the mid-1960s. Probably, George would have gained even more power nationally if he had not been paralyzed by an assassin's bullet during his 1972 presidential campaign. In his later years, after African-Americans began to vote in large numbers, he admitted that his racist politics had been a mistake, and, in 1986, he was named the best governor in the state's history, in a poll of Alabama blacks—all this for a governor who bellowed out in his 1963 inauguration speech, "I draw the line in the dust and toss the gauntlet before the feet of tyranny. And I say—segregation now, segregation tomorrow, segregation forever." Well, how the political winds do change.

## GEORGE WALLACE DOES
## THE DUMBEST THINGS

★ As a teenager, Wallace peddled magazines door to door. He sold subscriptions to nearly illiterate folks, telling them that he was from a fictional government agency, "the Bureau of Recapitulation and Matriculation," which required every American to read magazines. He even sold a subscription to a ninety-year-old blind woman.

★ In May 1963, the sheriff of Birmingham, Alabama, horrified America when he attacked civil rights protesters with powerful fire hoses and snarling dogs. Governor Wallace praised "the white people of Birmingham" for "their restraint during the present demonstrations."

★ Things got so violent in Birmingham that people began to refer to the town as Bombingham. In September 1963, Robert "Dynamite Bob" Chambliss and some of his Ku Klux Klan buddies reportedly bombed a local Baptist church, killing four young black girls. Wallace argued that it may not have been the work of white racists, explaining, "It could very easily have been done by communists or other Negroes who had a lot to gain by the ensuing publicity."

★ Before George stood in front of the doors of Foster Auditorium at the University of Alabama in June 1963 to protest the enrollment of two

Alabama governor George Wallace liked to ride around on caterpillars, but he hated "pointy-headed pseudo-intellectuals who can't park their bicycles straight."

(Courtesy of Bill Bridges/Archive Photos)

black students, his staff painted lines on the ground so that Wallace, the reporters, and the federal officials would know where to stand for the governor's historic display of obstructionism.

✪ In 1965, civil-rights marchers crossed over a bridge into Selma, Alabama, and were beaten by police for eighteen minutes in what one observer called "the most brutal scene I've ever witnessed." Commenting on the "Bloody Sunday" incident, Governor Wallace reasoned, "We saved lives by stopping that march. There's a good possibility that death would have resulted to some of those people if we had not stopped them."

✪ George Wallace could not legally succeed himself as governor in 1966, so instead his wife Lurleen ran and won the election. When she appeared before the joint legislature of Alabama to deliver her first speech, the lieutenant governor introduced her as "George Wallace."

✪ Wallace formed the American Independent Party in 1968 and ran for president. His vice presidential running mate for his 1968 campaign was the retired Air Force general Curtis LeMay. LeMay was a hawk on the Vietnam War, and threatened to "bomb them [the North Vietnamese] back into the Stone Age." LeMay told reporters he would use "nuclear weapons, if it was necessary" in Vietnam. Wallace and LeMay won five states and 13 percent of the popular vote in the 1968 presidential election.

★ In 1976 the wheelchair-bound Wallace made his third and last run for the presidency. "I'm not trying to compare myself with [Franklin] Roosevelt," Wallace declared, "but he couldn't walk either."

# Marion Zioncheck

## FACTS OF LIFE (and Death)

**ORIGIN:** Born Marion Anthony Zajaczek, December 5, 1901, Kety, Poland; died, August 7, 1936, Seattle, Washington. (Committed suicide by jumping out of an office building.)

**FORMATIVE YEARS:** University of Washington, J.D., 1928.

**FAMILY PLANNING:** Married Rubye Louise Nix (typist), 1935.

**SELECTED ELECTION SCORECARD:** 1932–34: won, U.S. House of Representatives, 1st District, Washington.

## QUICKIE BIO

"I am a radical and I'm damn proud of it. What do you think of that?" Marion Zioncheck was a real bohemian, born in the Bohemian region of Poland before his family brought him to the U.S. as a young child to grow up in Washington State. Zioncheck worked as a rat catcher, a cowboy, a lumberjack, and a fish peddler. He was elected president of the student body at the University of Washington, but annoyed so much of the student body that his classmates cut his hair and threw him in a lake. This should have been warning enough for the good people of Washington, but thirty-two-year-old Zioncheck was swept into Congress on FDR's coattails. Washington, D.C., drove the immigrant "Kid Congressman" crazy—literally.

# MARION ZIONCHECK DOES
# THE DUMBEST THINGS

✪ Brother "Z," as he was called, liked to drink absinthe and drive around the nation's capital in a big white Cadillac full of women. On such excursions he would yell, sing, and shout at passersby. Brother "Z" occasionally stopped his car, took off his pants and jumped into one of Washington's fountains.

✪ When Congressman Zioncheck finally decided to settle down, he drove with his fiancée to Maryland, borrowed the $2 fee from a court clerk, and got married. The newlyweds then returned to his Washington apartment where the groom dressed in an Indian outfit and posed with a bow and arrows for reporters. His wife explained that she hoped to reform him.

✪ In San Juan, Puerto Rico, for their honeymoon, Marion crashed a car into a truck, drove through a locked gate, barely escaped a duel, participated in "a riot for independence," phoned for the Marines, and threw coconuts from his hotel room onto an open dance floor below.

✪ Back in Washington, Zioncheck participated in the following exchange on the House floor with Rep. William Ekwall (R-Oregon)

> *Mr. Ekwall:* Mr. Speaker, I ask unanimous consent to address the House for five minutes.
>
> *Mr. Zioncheck:* Does the gentleman from Oregon wish to make a fool of himself?
>
> *Mr. Ekwall:* If anyone could make a bigger jackass of himself than the gentleman from Washington, I do not know who it is.

After the debate, a fellow congressman asked, "What is this, anyway? A kindergarten?"

✪ On New Year's Eve, 1935, young Congressman Zioncheck walked into a Washington apartment house, shoved aside the switchboard operator, plugged in every line in the building, and personally wished everyone "Happy New Year." Four policemen had to drag him from the building because he was so drunk he could not stand up. Declared Marion, "The police department is lousy."

✪ After being convicted of drunk and disorderly conduct, Zioncheck brought a copy of the court proceedings to the House and requested that the members vote unanimously to have the documents entered into the Congressional Record. As Marion explained, "I think you members of the House should know what is going on."

★ A few months later, Zioncheck got into an argument with Rep. Thomas L. Blanton (D-Texas) on the floor of the House. "The gentleman from Texas once said I was doped," Zioncheck declared. "And I shall put it into the record that the gentleman from Texas is a son of a Texan. On second thought I'll revise my remark and leave a blank for the final word." Blanton lunged at Zioncheck, but the other House members held him back. The House voted 274–0 to expunge Marion's remarks.

★ Zioncheck bought a new car, and enjoyed speeding through traffic lights and driving on the left side of the road. Arrested for speeding at seventy-five miles per hour through the streets of Washington, the politician defended himself by saying, "It couldn't have been me. I was doing eighty-five."

★ Marion failed to appear in court to answer the speeding charges. When a police sergeant appeared at the House of Representatives office building to arrest Zioncheck, the legislator claimed that he could not be arrested on federal property because of federal immunity. He then decided to cooperate, jumped into his car and zipped off toward the courthouse. After driving for a few blocks, Marion changed his mind again, jumped out of the car, and ran back to the House office building. The police officer chased after Zioncheck, yelling at him to "act like a gentleman." Marion retorted, "Take off you glasses and draw your gun." The two wrestled, and Zioncheck injured the policeman before District of Columbia police grabbed him and hauled the congressman into the guardroom.

★ Zioncheck finally agreed to go to court to answer the charges leveled against him. He represented himself, and pleaded guilty, but said he hadn't been properly notified about the charges. "Just a minute," Marion challenged when the judge retired to his chambers to think about his argument, "what about my case?" "The court is recessing," the judge said. "I'm taking a recess too," Zioncheck shouted, and ran for the door.

★ Officers threw Zioncheck into a cell, where he spent two hours making faces for photographers, climbing up the bars, and poking out his hat, begging for funds while demanding that the Speaker of the House get him out of jail on the grounds of congressional immunity. The House decided to pay the initial fine and all additional ones the court levied against Zioncheck. The politician triumphantly told the press that he was returning to his apartment to look after his four pet turtles. One of his fellow congressmen suggested that he see a therapist.

- When his landlady asked for the rent, Marion assaulted her, and was finally committed to an institution for the mentally disturbed. But Zioncheck climbed a seven-foot fence, ran through the woods, and made his way back to the House office building. As long as he was there, the head of the Capitol Police (the federal force who guard federal government buildings) and the sergeant-at-arms of the House refused to let Zioncheck be taken back into custody, claiming that while he remained on the Capitol grounds, only the special congressional police could arrest him. The standoff became known as "the Zioncheck problem."

- Zioncheck was finally persuaded to leave the Capitol area and return to his hometown of Seattle. As he left, Marion refused to wave farewell to reporters, and warned, "I'll be back."

- Zioncheck never did go back to Congress. Instead, he committed suicide by jumping out of the window of a Seattle office building. The man who was driven insane by Republicans and Democrats left behind a scrawled suicide note that read, "My only hope in life was to improve the condition of an unfair economic system. . . ."

# THE
# THIRD-PARTY
# POLITICIANS

# Ross Perot

## FACTS OF LIFE

**ORIGIN:** Born Henry Ray Perot (changed his name to Henry Ross at the age of twelve), June 27, 1930, Texarkana, Texas.

**FORMATIVE YEARS:** Attended Texarkana Community College for two years, in 1949 transferred to the U.S. Naval Academy, graduated 1953.

**FAMILY PLANNING:** Married Margot Birmingham (teacher), September 13, 1956.

**SELECTED ELECTION SCORECARD:** 1992: lost, U.S. president. 1996: lost, U.S. president.

## QUICKIE BIO

Good guys don't necessarily finish first," billionaire Ross Perot declared, "and the world is not a fair place." Ross Perot was not a typical "good guy," and he did not finish first, at least in presidential elections. Born to a cotton broker in East Texas, young Perot earned spending money by breaking wild horses and delivering papers on horseback. Ambitious, competitive, and short, Perot became a naval officer, then quit to join IBM. Perot worked as a "salesman for IBM for five years, then formed his own company, Electronic Data Systems (EDS). Ross got the data processing contract for Medicare and Medicaid and was dubbed America's first "welfare billionaire." Described by journalists as an "elf with [a] banana nose and [a] putting green hairdo," Perot sold his company for $2.5 billion, and chose to run for president in

1992 as an Independent. Speaking bottom-linese in a high nasal voice, he wowed dissatisfied voters and won 19 percent of the votes for president, more than any third party candidate since 1912. He founded the Reform Party in 1996, and ran again for president in that year. However, by that time the public apparently had tired of his paranoia, his egotism, and his annoying voice. He received only 8 percent of the vote in 1996, and then was engulfed in a furious political battle for control of the party he had started, primarily against the new governor of Minnesota, Jesse "The Body" Ventura, who had won that office as an Independent. Ross's well-touted motto was, "To know me is to love me."

## ROSS PEROT DOES
## THE DUMBEST THINGS

✪ Ross met Margot Birmingham, his future wife, on a blind date in October 1952. Perot claimed, "It was love at first sight." Margot told a friend after the date, "Well, he was clean."

✪ As the only sailor who "didn't drink, didn't swear, and didn't mess around with women," Perot didn't think much of his mates in the U.S. Navy. He described them as "tattooed and drunk." He got an early discharge from the service. During his presidential campaign, he claimed that he left the seafaring service because his father was ill. At other times he claimed that he quit the navy because he objected to the seniority system. At one point, Perot insisted that it was all a misunderstanding as to the reason for his return to civilian life.

✪ In 1965, Ross hired a former IBM lobbyist to start EDS's first satellite office in Washington, D.C., and lobby for lucrative government contracts. Perot even lobbied for himself on occasion. In 1972, he met with Caspar Weinberger, Secretary of Health, Education, and Welfare, and demanded to be given the data processing contracts for Medicare. "I gave five million bucks to Nixon," Perot reportedly reasoned, "and I want that contract now!" He did not get the deal.

✪ During his first presidential bid, Ross changed his mind about lobbyists and claimed "they are really hurting this country."

✪ In the late 1960s Ross became a big booster of President Nixon. Supposedly, he promised $10 million to set up a pro-Nixon think tank and $50 million for media exposure, but never came forth with the funding. Special presidential counsel Charles Colson described it as "one of the most effective con jobs I ever saw in the White House."

★ After he launched a campaign to help the prisoners of war (POWs) and the missing in action (MIAs) in Vietnam, Ross claimed that the North Vietnamese had targeted him for assassination and had hired the Black Panthers to carry out the task. Perot insisted that one night he saw "five people coming across my front lawn with rifles." According to the Texan, his guard dog bit a "big piece out of the seat of one of the guys as he went over the fence. We thought we would be able to find that person, because if you take a tremendous hit to your seat, you bleed profusely." Perot's security guards claimed no knowledge of such an attack.

★ In 1981, Perot supported soldier of fortune "Bo" Gritz on a mission to Southeast Asia to search for POWs. "And I'm not interested in bones," Ross said. Gritz went to Southeast Asia, and claimed that he found POWs. His evidence? Bones. Unfortunately they were chicken bones. "I know a chicken bone," Gritz said in his own defense. "I eat a lot of Kentucky Fried Chicken."

★ In the late 1970s, Perot worked on an anti-drug task force for the state of Texas. He became convinced that he was going to be assassinated by the father of actor Woody Harrelson (*Cheers*) and assembled a security team to follow the elder Harrelson.

★ Ross hired former U.S. military counter-terrorist commandos to combat drugs smuggled into the United States and offered to buy a Caribbean island to set up an elaborate drug sting operation. In exchange, he wanted the exclusive contract to supply the island with gas and other services, "If I'm going to buy a damn island down there, I want my money back."

★ In December 1978, two top EDS executives were arrested in Iran. Perot called Henry Kissinger, Alexander Haig, and other high members of President Nixon's White House team to get help. After three days, he took matters into his own hands and created Operation Hotfoot (Help Our Two Friends Out of Tehran) to bust his employees out of prison. Tom Luce, his lawyer, called the plan "idiotic." Ross flew his crack team (the "Sunshine Boys") to Tehran, where they booked into the local Hyatt Hotel and spent their time studying the situation by watching TV. Meanwhile, rioting Iranian mobs stormed the prison and released all the prisoners. Perot's two freed employees hitchhiked to the Hyatt in Tehran. Ross later told reporters that the two executives had fled "through intense gunfire for about two miles on foot" and claimed that his squad was responsible for the escape.

"The planet is our home," the diminutive billionaire Ross Perot decreed. "If we destroy the planet, we've destroyed our home, so it is fundamentally important."
(Courtesy of Reuters/Peter Morgan/Archive Photos)

★ Ross paid best-selling novelist Ken Follett to write a book about the incident entitled *On Wings of Eagles* (1983), which was later made into a TV miniseries. Perot confessed that the action-packed, violent television offering deviated from the real story. "The biggest changes were: We didn't kill anybody . . ."

★ Ross later sold EDS to General Motors. Soon after, he began talking about "nuking" GM. The conglomerate offered Perot $700 million just to go away. "Why should I take this money?" the entrepreneur asked. "It would be morally wrong. I don't need it." Eventually, he accepted the funds.

★ During the 1992 presidential campaign, third-party candidate Perot promised to "get under the hood" of the national economy and said that the national debt was like a "crazy aunt in the basement." How to fix health care? "We will take it apart." He proposed a fifty cent a gallon gasoline tax, and promised to solve the deficit problem "without breaking a sweat." Mort Meyerson, his campaign manager, observed, "I could care less about politics. I rarely read a newspaper and I don't vote."

★ During a presidential debate with Democratic candidate Bill Clinton and Pres. George Bush, big-eared Perot piped up, "I'm all ears."

- Perot dropped out of the presidential race in July 1992. Mort Meyerson was relieved that he "didn't have to continue going on the death march." But in late September 1992, Perot jumped back into the race. He claimed that he had quit because the Republicans were planning to disrupt his daughter's wedding.

- As the election results came in, Perot and his wife had a party and danced to the Patsy Cline song "Crazy." Ross explained, "The devil made me do it."

# Jesse Ventura

## FACTS OF LIFE

**ORiGiN:** Born James George Janos, July 15, 1951, Minneapolis, Minnesota. (He later had his name legally changed to Jesse Ventura, and copyrighted it.)

**FORMATiVE YEARS:** Attended North Hennepin Community College for one year (1975), but dropped out to become a professional wrestler.

**FAMiLY PLANNiNG:** Married Terry Larson (horse trainer), July 18, 1975.

**SELECTED ELECTiON SCORECARD:** 1998: won, governor, Minnesota.

## QUICKIE BIO

I'm not a Democrat," Jesse "The Body" Ventura declared, "I'm not a Republican." But when he announced, "I'm Czech!" his aunt corrected him: "You are not! You're Slovak!" A self-described "six-foot-four, 250-pound ex–Navy SEAL, pro wrestler, radio personality, and film actor," James Janos was born into a working class family in Minnesota. After serving in the military he joined a motorcycle gang and met his future wife while he was working as a bouncer at a biker bar. Searching for a career path, Janos chose professional wrestling. He was a big fan of "Superstar" Billy Graham, so he dyed his hair blond and set out to be a bad guy. He started out as "Janos the Dirty," then "Surfer" Jesse Ventura, then Jesse

"The Body" Ventura. After he suffered pulmonary emboli in 1986, "The Body" became "The Mouth," as he quit wrestling to become a commentator and talk-radio host. He ran for mayor of his hometown, Brooklyn Park, Minnesota, after he got mad at developers who wanted to put in sidewalks and sewers. Later he got angry again, and decided to join the Reform Party and run for governor of Minnesota. He won the election, with the largest voter turnout in Minnesota's history. How did he do it? "The bottom line is that my opponents were boring." And what was one of the first political acts of the feather boa–wearing wrestler who once had referred to government as "cancer" and dubbed himself "Governor Klingon"? He tried to get his wife on the state payroll.

## JESSE VENTURA DOES THE DUMBEST THINGS

✪ For years Ventura went for an annual "fishing" trip with his pals. They didn't do much fishing, but they did party in mobile homes with stereos and lots of fireworks and booze. Ventura explained, "It's roughing it. It's Minnesotan. It's the kind of trip where every waking moment you have a beer in your hand."

✪ As a wrestling bad guy, Jesse admitted, "It was usually my job to lose." However, he still claimed that this fact "in no way means it's fake."

✪ Jesse formed a rock band called Soldiers of Fortune, but admitted, "I really don't know whether or not we sucked. . . ."

✪ In his early days as a radio talk-show host, Jesse called one of his guests a "little commie," then, later apologized, and called the whole thing "stupid."

✪ Ventura criticized his gubernatorial opponents by saying, "Most of them wouldn't know crime if it came up and bit 'em on the a**." But when asked about what he would do about crime as governor, Ventura answered, "Nothing!"

✪ Ventura on the death penalty: "We don't have it here in Minnesota, thank God, and I won't advocate to get it." But he added, "There's another part of me that hears about these brutal mass murderers and thinks, Gee, maybe I'd like to walk over and pull the switch. Would that be a hands-on governor?"

✪ Jesse admitted that he did drugs beginning in high school, and justified his indulgence by explaining, "Back then, drugs were not a business, they were anti-establishment and provided escape." What is his answer to the drug problem today? "Let's regulate it!"

⭐ When asked if he supported legalizing pot, Jesse straddled the issue. "Let's not talk about whether to make it legal or illegal, let's talk about the monetary potential."

⭐ As a young man, Ventura enjoyed the company of hookers. "Incredible," he said, of Nevada brothels. "You go down the line, they each tell you their name, and you pick out the one you want. In those days it was cheap—ten to fifteen bucks." But not cheap enough for Jesse. He traded one prostitute a belt he had made from empty shell casings, for sexual favors *and* ten dollars. "I'm probably one of the only people in the world who's gone into a Nevada ranch and been paid. I used that ten dollars to go to another one."

⭐ When he became governor he described prostitutes as a "social problem" and a "consensual crime." How best to fight it? According to Governor Ventura, "Volunteering."

⭐ While he was a Navy SEAL, Jesse joined the anti–Vietnam War movement. Why? "I loved the braless thing. I'm very heterosexual. I'd see women out burning their bras and I'd go over with a lighter: 'Can I help?'"

"Organized religion is a sham and a crutch for weak-minded people who need strength in numbers," Jesse Ventura observed in *Playboy* magazine. He later claimed that being weak-minded was "not necessarily a detriment" and described his own wife as weak-minded because she went to church.

(Courtesy of Reuters/Eric Miller/Archive Photos)

★ What did Ventura claim he would like to be reincarnated as? A size 38DD bra.

★ Jesse felt as strongly about gun control people as he felt about bras. "Gun control people don't know what they're talking about," he declared. "They're ignorant."

★ An avid conspiracy fan, Ventura liked to quote rock singer Jim Morrison and claimed that he wanted to retire to Hawaii and be a beach bum, saying, "It worked for Jim Morrison, didn't it?" Wrong: Jim Morrison of the Doors died of a heart attack in France.

★ The first lady of Minnesota, Terry Ventura, declared, "I'm not stupid. I went to Wendy Ward Charm School at Ward's when I was thirteen, excuse me. I know how to walk, how to get in and out of a car without showing the world everything."

# BiBLiOGRAPHY

## SELECTED PERIODICALS

*Austin-American Statesman*          *The New Yorker*
*Boston Globe*                       *Newsweek*
*Current Biography*                  *Official Congressional Directory*
*The Drudge Report*                  *People*
*The Flynt Report*                   *Sacramento Bee*
*George*                             *Slate*
*Globe*                              *Spy*
*GQ*                                 *Star*
*Houston Chronicle*                  *Talk*
*Houston Press*                      *Time*
*Los Angeles Times*                  *USA Today*
*Mother Jones*                       *Vanity Fair*
*National Enquirer*                  *Wall Street Journal*
*New York Times*                     *Washington Post*

## BOOKS

Adler, Bill. *The Wit and Wisdom of Jimmy Carter.* Secaucus, NJ: Citadel Press, 1977.

Agronsky, Jonathan I. Z. *Marion Barry: The Politics of Race.* Latham, NY: British American Publishing, 1991.

Allen, Jessica. *The Wit and Wisdom of Jesse "The Body . . . The Mind" Ventura.* New York: William Morrow, 1999.

Barone, Michael, and Grant Ujifusa with Richard E. Cohen. *The Almanac of American Politics 1998.* Washington, D.C.: National Journal, 1998.

Barras, Jonetta Rose. *The Last of the Black Emperors: The Hollow Comeback of Marion Barry in the New Age of Black Leadership.* Baltimore, MD: Bancroft Press, 1998.

Beatty, Jack. *The Rascal King: The Life and Times of James Michael Curley (1874–1958).* Boston, MA: Addison-Wesley, 1992.

Belsky, Gary. *On Second Thought: 365 of the Worst Promises, Predictions, and Pronouncements Ever Made!!!* Holbrook, MA: Adams Media Corporation, 1999.

Beschloss, Michael R. *Taking Charge: The Johnson White House Tapes, 1963–1964.* New York: Simon and Schuster, 1997.

Bly, Nellie. *The Kennedy Men: Three Generations of Sex, Scandal, and Secrets.* New York: Kensington Books, 1996.

Boller, Paul F., Jr. *Congressional Anecdotes.* Oxford, England: Oxford University Press, 1991.

———. *Presidential Anecdotes.* New York: Penguin Books, 1986.

Bowles, Billy, and Remer Tyson. *They Love a Man in the Country: Saints and Sinners in the South.* Atlanta, GA: Peachtree Publishers, 1989.

Brallier, Jess, and Sally Chabert. *Presidential Wit and Wisdom: Maxims, Mottoes, Sound Bites, Speeches, and Asides.* London, England: Penguin Books, 1996.

Cawthorne, Nigel. *Sex Lives of the Presidents.* New York: St. Martin's Press, 1998.

Cockburn, Alexander, and Ken Silverstein. *Washington Babylon.* New York: Verso, 1996.

David, Lester. *Good Ted, Bad Ted: The Two Faces of Edward M. Kennedy.* New York: Carol Publishing, 1993.

Davis, Kenneth C. *Don't Know Much About History.* New York: Avon Books, 1990.

Duncan, Philip D., and Brian Nutting, editors. *CQ's Politics in America 2000: The 106th Congress.* Washington, D.C.: Congressional Quarterly, 1999.

Ford, Gerald R. *Humor and the Presidency.* New York: Arbor House, 1987.

Frady, Marshall. *Jesse: The Life and Pilgrimage of Jesse Jackson.* New York: Random House, 1996.

Garment, Suzanne. *Scandal: The Culture of Mistrust in American Politics.* New York: Times Books, 1991.

Gregory, Leland H., III. *Great Government Goofs! Over 350 Loopy Laws, Hilarious Screwups, and Acts-idents of Congress.* New York: Dell, 1997.

———. *Presidential Indiscretions.* New York: Dell Trade Paperback, 1999.

Hagood, Wesley O. *Presidential Sex: From the Founding Fathers to Bill Clinton.* New York: Citadel Press, 1995.

Hair, Vivian Ivy. *The Kingfish and His Realm: The Life and Times of Huey P. Long.* Baton Rouge: Louisiana State University Press, 1991.

Haygood, Wil. *King of the Cats: The Life and Times of Adam Clayton Powell, Jr.* New York: Houghton Mifflin, 1993.

Hersh, Burton. *The Shadow President: Ted Kennedy in Opposition.* South Royalton, VT: Steerforth Press, 1997.

Hersch, Seymour. *The Dark Side of Camelot.* New York: Little, Brown, 1997.

Holli, Melvin G. *The American Mayor: The Best and the Worst Big-City Leaders.* University Park, PA: Pennsylvania State University Press, 1999.

Isikoff, Michael. *Uncovering Clinton.* New York: Crown, 1999.

Jackley, John L. *Below the Beltway.* New York: Regnery, 1996.

Jenrette, Rita. *My Capitol Secrets.* New York: Bantam, 1981.

Kane, Joseph Nathan. *Presidential Fact Book.* New York: Random House, 1998.

Kaptor, Marcy, ed. *Women of Congress: A Twentieth Century Odyssey.* Washington, D.C.: Congressional Quarterly, 1996.

Killian, Linda. *The Freshmen: Whatever Happened to the Republican Revolution?* Boulder, CO.: Westview, 1998.

Klein, Edward. *All Too Human: The Love Story of Jack and Jackie Kennedy.* New York: Ballantine, 1996

———.*Just Jackie.* New York: Ballantine, 1998.

Koch, Edward I., with William Rauch. *Mayor.* New York: Simon and Schuster, 1984.

Kohn, George C. *Encyclopedia of American Scandal.* New York: Facts on File, 1989.

Kohut, John J. *Stupid Government Tricks.* New York: Plume, 1995.

Kohut, John J., and Roland Sweet. *Dumb, Dumber, Dumbest: True News of the World's Least Competent People.* New York: Plume, 1996.

———.*More Dumb, Dumber, Dumbest: True News of the World's Least Competent People.* New York: Plume, 1998.

Kurtz, Michael L., and Morgan D. Peoples. *Earl K. Long: The Saga of Uncle Earl and Louisiana Politics.* Baton Rouge, LA: Louisiana State University Press, 1990.

Lesher, Stephan. *George Wallace: American Populist.* Reading, MA: Addison-Wesley Publishing, 1993.

Liebman, Glenn. *Political Shorts: 1,001 of the Funniest Political One-Liners.* Chicago, IL: Contemporary Books, 1999.

Maraniss, David. *First in His Class: A Biography of Bill Clinton.* New York: Simon and Schuster, 1995.

McMullan, Jim. *Hail to the Chief.* Los Angeles, CA: General Publishing Group, 1996.

Milton, Joyce. *First Partner: Hillary Rodham Clinton.* New York: William Morrow, 1999.

Morris, Roger. *Partners in Power.* New York: Henry Holt, 1996.

O'Brien, Steven G. *American Political Leaders: From Colonial Times to the Present.* Santa Barbara, CA: ABC-CLIO, 1991.

Olive, David. *More Political Babble.* New York: John Wiley and Sons, 1996.

———. *Political Babble: The 1,000 Dumbest Things Ever Said by Politicians.* New York: John Wiley and Sons, 1992.

Petras, Ross, and Kathryn Petras. *The 365 Stupidest Things Ever Said.* New York: Workman Publishing, 1997.

Powell, Adam Clayton, Jr. *Adam by Adam: The Autobiography of Adam Clayton Powell, Jr.* New York: The Dial Press, 1971.

Rapoport, Roger. *California Dreaming: The Political Odyssey of Pat and Jerry Brown.* Berkeley, CA: Nolo Press, 1982.

Ross, Shelley. *Fall from Grace: Sex, Scandal, and Corruption in American Politics from 1702 to the Present.* New York: Ballantine Books, 1988.

Schell, Orville. *Brown.* New York: Random House, 1978.

Sharpton, Al, and Anthony Walton. *Go and Tell Pharoah: The Autobiography of the Reverend Al Sharpton.* New York: Doubleday, 1996.

Slansky, Paul. *The Clothes Have No Emperor: A Chronicle of the American 80s.* New York: Simon and Schuster, 1989.

Strausbaugh, John. *Alone with the President.* New York: Blast Books, 1993.

Tally, Steve. *Bland Ambition: From Adams to Quayle—the Cranks, Criminals, Tax Cheats, and Golfers Who Made It to Vice President.* New York: Harcourt Brace Jovanovich, 1992.

Taylor, Glen H. *The Way It Was With Me.* New York: Lyle Stuart, 1979.

Udall, Morris K. *Too Funny to Be President.* New York: Henry Holt, 1988.

Ventura, Jesse. *I Ain't Got Time to Bleed: Reworking the Body Politic from the Bottom Up.* New York: Villard, 1999.

*Who's Who in American Politics 1997–1998.* New Providence, NY: Marquis Who's Who, 1998.

Wicker, Tom. *One of Us: Richard Nixon and the American Dream.* New York: Random House, 1991.

Williams, T. Harry. *Huey Long.* New York: Vintage, 1969.

## WEB REFERENCE SITES

Official Web sites of various politicians usually only provide limited biographical information along with selected speeches and press releases—boring. Most anti-candidate Internet sites ignore the good dumb stuff in favor of polemics. Below I have listed those sites I found most useful in compiling this book, but if you find any additional good ones, let us know and we'll post them at our own Web site: www.dumbest.com. (Please note that Internet Web sites frequently change their URL addresses.)

### For basic biographical information on Congress and the president:
bioguide.congress.gov/biosearch/biosearch.asp
www.capweb.net
www.vote-smart.org

### For information on selected politicians:
House of Crooks (www.sit.wisc.edu/~lsfitzge)

### For information on presidential candidates:
Skeleton Closet (www.realchange.org)

### For information on Bill Clinton and the women in his life:
www.comedyontap.com/presgirls.html

# INDEX

# ABOUT THE AUTHOR

**Bill Crawford** first got involved in politics as an elementary-school student, when he volunteered for the 1968 George Wallace presidential campaign. If that wasn't dumb enough, he graduated from Phillips Academy, Andover, earned a degree in the study of religion from Harvard University, got an M.B.A. from the University of Texas at Austin, and started writing books. Crawford has written for the *Austin Chronicle, Texas Monthly, Oklahoma Today*, and a number of other publications. He is the author of *Republicans Do the Dumbest Things* (Renaissance, 2000) and co-author of five previous books, including *Stevie Ray Vaughan: Caught in the Crossfire* (Little, Brown, 1993), *Rock Stars Do the Dumbest Things* (Renaissance, 1998), *Movie Stars Do the Dumbest Things* (Renaissance, 1999), and *Border Radio*. Crawford lives in Austin, Texas, with his wife and two children, who all play soccer while he drinks tequila.

# Also Available From Renaissance Books

BOOKS